COOKIE'S DEDICATION

There are so many people who have supported the original BEAUTIFUL BUFFETS over the years, but the choice was clear when I thought about the dedication for this 25th anniversary edition.

I want to honor the memory of my late husband, Barry Stagman, who was the heart and soul of my first book. He was the inspiration for so much that happened in our lives. I miss his energy and his positive attitude. He lived his life from a place of great love for his family and his friends.

I know Barry would want to share this "dedication" with our 5 grandchildren: Carly, Maya, Logan, Danielle and Lindsee. They love baking with me, their Nana, and really enjoy eating all the goodies. They are truly the "sweetness" in my life.

. . . .

ARLENE'S DEDICATION

25 years ago, my husband Keith and our three children, Scott, Jaime and Hawkeye were frequent "tasters" for the original book. For this edition, Keith was a very willing participant. Scott's wife Liza, and their four children, Cameron, Dylan, Zoey and Hailey were very helpful in testing and tasting. My daughter Jaime did lots of testing and her new husband, Bryan Olson, did lots of "tasting"! Our son Hawkeye is always a willing food taster and critic. It became a wonderful family project!

I dedicate this book to my family's willingness to always support my efforts both in and out of the kitchen. They are the true blessings in my life!

WITH SPECIAL THANKS...

TO ALL THE TALENTED AMERICAN DESIGNERS WHO CONTRIBUTED TO THIS BOOK:

Becky Bisoulis

Bill Blass

Eleanor P. Brenner

Oscar De La Renta

Louis Dell'Olio

James Galanos

Mark Heister

Caroline Herrera

Donna Karan

Barry Kieselstein-Cord

CeCe Cord

Adrienne Landau

Ann Lawrence

Judith Leiber

Bob Mackie

Isaac Mizrahi

Nancy and David

Albert and Pearl Nipon

Maria Rodriguez

Carolyne Roehm

Sandra Roth

Arnold Scaasi

TO ALL THE WONDERFUL PEOPLE WHO TESTED BEAUTIFUL BUFFETS, II AND GAVE ME GREAT SUGGESTIONS:

Sandy Brand

Jaime Bronstein Olson

Liza Bronstein

Debbie Goodman

Logan Hacking

Debbi Klein

Karen Lee

Laurie Ringel

Joanne Savage

Hadas Stagman

Marley Stein

Robin Stern

Liz Weiser

Lynnie White

AND A SPECIAL THANK YOU TO **ARIELLE MATLIN**, WHO HELPED PUT TOGETHER BEAUTIFUL BUFFETS II. SHE IS VERY ORGANIZED AND PATIENT, AND MADE THE WHOLE PROCESS LOTS OF FUN!

FRONT AND BACK COVER PHOTOS BY RICHARD SHAY:
RICHARD SHAY PHOTOGRAPHY GLENCOE, ILLINOIS

A PORTION OF THE PROCEEDS OF THIS COOKBOOK GOES TO
THE LYNN SAGE CANCER RESEARCH FOUNDATION

TABLE OF CONTENTS

INTRODUCTION

I t's hard to believe that it has been 25 years since we first published BEAUTIFUL BUFFETS. At the time, my husband Barry and I were in the fashion business. We were partners in every sense of the word. We were the showroom for many of the most prominent designers in the country. People from all over the States would come to our showroom to order for their stores. We had buyers from the biggest department stores to the smallest boutiques. Somewhere around 1985, the Apparel Mart was created in Chicago. Barry was a terrific entrepreneur and he wanted something that would make our showroom unique. I really loved to cook and thought it would give our space a very special touch to have home-cooked foods, rather than the catered affairs others would bring in. It didn't take long for word to spread that we were serving the best food in town.

The food became so popular, that many of the buyers began requesting recipes. It was always my pleasure. I loved hearing how they enjoyed sharing their new taste treats with their family and friends. After a couple of years of printing hundreds of recipes, Barry decided, we should do a cookbook. Needless to say, cooking and baking is one thing. Writing a book was quite another!

Barry and I had gone to college with Arlene Bronstein. Although she had never written a cookbook, we knew that she had organized many activities in our home-town of Glencoe Illinois and we knew she was resourceful. We pitched her the thought, and she loved the idea of "quick and easy" recipes. We both had young children at the time and didn't have a lot of time to prepare home-cooked meals.

The book became a real labor of love. For over a year, Arlene tweaked the recipes in her kitchen and then asked many friends and family members to try them in their home kitchens. The "testers" encouraged us to move forward. They said the recipes were easy to prepare and delicious to eat! And so the book was born. BEAUTIFUL BUFFETS sold over 20,000 copies. That is an incredible amount for what was a labeled a "local cookbook". But thanks to Neiman Marcus and Saks Fifth Avenue, that "local" label became a nationwide success. We were also supported by our many fashion boutiques all over the country. The book sold in local bookshops, through the big chains like Kroch's and Brentanos and in small food emporiums like Sunset Foods. Every one of the book-signings featured free samples. The "tastings" sold the book. After three printings, the original BEAUTIFUL BUFFETS went out of print. Amazon still had access to books, but the prices were staggering. One sold for $168.00. Others found the book at Flea Markets and paid $5.00 and thought they had "scored" a treasure.

In the years since the book was published, I haven't stopped cooking and creating. I really love to be in the kitchen. It makes me so happy to watch people enjoy what I have made. I still use my mother's original cookie cutters and my mother wasn't even a cook, but her home was warm and loving. I think of my parents, Regina and Fred Jawer almost every day. Everyone loved to come to their home. Once I had my own home, I wanted it to feel like theirs. I know that my kitchens...no matter if they are in Illinois or Florida, they are places where people can feel comfortable talking about their happiness or sharing their sadness. Barry wanted to have a sign printed that read: Cookie Stagman, Personal Counselor.

So, even though it has been 25 years since BEAUTIFUL BUFFETS was published, it still makes me happy to share my recipes. I have updated the original book with new measurements, ingredients and can sizes where needed. I have also chosen 40 of my favorite new recipes. These recipes will be denoted with "FORKS". Like the recipes in the original BEAUTIFUL BUFFETS, these are quick and easy and so yummy. I hope you will have fun in your kitchen creating these treats. And I hope that your kitchen will be a place where family and friends like to gather. My biggest happiness is cooking for my children, Jason and his wife Hadas and my daughter Lizie and her husband Larry Lazar and their children, my fiancé Gary and my wonderful friends who are "the family" I have chosen! Enjoy!

My best to you,

Cookie

SOME HELPFUL HINTS

EMERGENCY SUBSTITUTIONS

Sometimes you're in the mood to cook and you realize that you are out of the specified ingredients. This chart has helped me and I hope it will be of use to you, too.

IF A RECIPE CALLS FOR: USE INSTEAD:

IF A RECIPE CALLS FOR:	USE INSTEAD:
1 cup of catsup or chili sauce	1 cup tomato sauce plus ½ cup sugar and 2 tablespoons of vinegar
1 small onion	1 tablespoon of dried minced onions
1 tablespoon of any fresh herbs	1 teaspoon of dried herbs
1 ounce unsweetened chocolate	3 tablespoons cocoa plus 1 tablespoon butter
1 whole egg	3 egg yolks
1 teaspoon dry mustard	1 tablespoon prepared mustard
1 clove garlic	⅛ teaspoon garlic powder
1 cup tomato juice	½ cup tomato sauce plus ½ cup water
1 cup sour milk or buttermilk	1 tablespoon lemon juice or vinegar, plus sweetened condensed milk to equal 1 cup (let stand 5 minutes)
1 cup whole milk	½ cup evaporated milk plus ½ cup water or 1 cup dry non-fat milk plus 2½ teaspoons butter
1 cup cake flour	1 cup minus 2 tablespoons all purpose flour
1 stick of sweet butter	use 1 stick of regular butter and leave out ½ of the salt ingredient required

INSTANT EQUIVALENTS

BUTTER AND CHOCOLATE

2 tablespoons butter = 1 ounce
1 stick of butter = ½ cup
1 square of chocolate = 1 ounce

CRUMBS

14 squares of graham crackers = 1 cup fine crumbs
19 chocolate wafers = 1 cup fine crumbs
1 slice bread, dried = ⅓ cup
4 ounce potato chips = 2 cups coarsely chopped

FRUITS AND VEGETABLES

Juice of 1 lemon = about 3 tablespoons
Grated peel of lemon = about 1 teaspoon
Juice of 1 orange = about ⅓ cup
Grated peel of orange = about 2 teaspoons
1 medium apple, chopped = about 1 cup
1 medium onion, chopped = about ½ cup
1 15-ounce box of raisins = 3 cups

CREAM, CHEESE AND EGGS

1 cup whipping cream = 2 cups whipped
1 pound American cheese = 4 cups shredded
¼ pound blue cheese = ½ cup crumbled
12-14 egg yolks = 1 cup
8-10 egg whites = 1 cup

NUTS

1 pound walnuts in shell = about 1½ to 1 ¾ cups shelled
1 pound almonds in shell = ¾ to 1 cup shelled

CREAM

½ pint sour cream = 1 cup
½ pound cottage cheese = 1 cup

SOME HANDY MEASUREMENTS

Dash = less then ⅛ teaspoon

3 teaspoons = 1 tablespoon

4 tablespoons = ¼ cup

5⅓ tablespoons = ⅓ cup

8 tablespoons = ½ cup

10⅔ tablespoons = ⅔ cup

12 tablespoons = ¾ cup

16 tablespoons = 1 cup

1 cup = 8 fluid ounces

1 cup = ½ pint

2 cups = 1 pint

4 cups = 1 quart

4 quarts = 1 gallon

8 quarts = 1 peck

4 pecks = 1 bushel

1 liter = 1.06 quarts

COOKIE'S COOKIES

COOKIE'S COOKIES

COOKIE'S COOKIE TIPS

1. Check your oven temperature. You would be surprised how "Off" it can be. Have it professionally calibrated.
2. Use only the freshest ingredients!
3. I use Grade A large eggs.
4. Always use the finest quality pure vanilla extract.
5. If the recipe calls for sweet butter and you only have salted, just reduce the amount of salt called for the in the recipe or eliminate the salt completely.
6. Even when a recipe doesn't call for "greasing" a cookie sheet, I spray them anyway.
7. I bake my cookies on large, aluminum oven liners. If I bake smaller batches, I use regular shiny aluminum cookie sheets. Today I always use parchment paper to line the cookie sheets.
8. I use 2 teaspoons for drop cookies. I scoop with one and push the dough off onto the pan with the other.
9. Always leave 3 inches between cookies. Most cookies spread a little.
10. For more uniform cookies, use a small ice cream scoop.
11. "Confectioners sugar" and "Powdered sugar" are the same thing. When using it as a garnish, I put it in a small can with a strainer on top and then shake it to lightly dust the cookies or bars.
12. Do not over bake cookies! They become hard and dry. Better to under bake them and you'll have a moister, chewier cookie. Each oven is different (about a 25 degree variation) so watch the progress through the oven window. Opening the oven door can distort the cooking process.
13. Most of my cookies can be made ahead of time and frozen. I use heavy plastic containers or tin cans with airtight lids. I line the bottom with wax paper and put it between the layers of cookies, too.
14. It is best to freeze each type of cookie separately so they don't take on other flavors. As cookies defrost, they contain a different amount of moisture and this may change the texture of some cookies.

CANDY BAR COOKIES

A child's delight, but oh how my buyers love them! These cookies freeze beautifully, and look as good as they taste! I often double this recipe.

YIELD: 20 -25 COOKIES   PREHEAT OVEN TO 350 DEGREES

- ½ cup sugar
- ½ cup brown sugar, packed
- ½ cup butter
- ½ cup peanut butter
- 1 teaspoon vanilla extract
- 1 egg
- 1½ cups flour
- ½ teaspoon baking powder
- ½ teaspoon baking soda
- 10-15 small Snicker or Milky Way Candy Bars (I split them in half)
- 20-25 wooden sucker sticks

In a large bowl, combine sugar, brown sugar, butter, peanut butter, vanilla extract and egg. Beat well. Add flour, baking powder and baking soda. Mix well. Cut candy bars in half and insert a stick to form a lollipop. Wrap enough dough around the candy bar to cover completely.

Place on a cookie sheet sprayed with non-stick cooking spray. Bake in a preheated 350 degree oven until light brown; about 12 minutes. Cool 10 minutes and remove from cookie sheet.

P.S. Recently, many of the candy companies have come out with mini versions in bags. They are fantastic and don't even need unwrapping!

PEANUT BUTTER DOODLES

This recipe was requested by the Chicago Sun-Times. It's a real favorite!

YIELD: 40   PREHEAT OVEN TO 350 DEGREES

- ½   cup butter
- ½   cup peanut butter
- ½   cup sugar
- ½   cup brown sugar
- 1   egg
- 1   teaspoon vanilla extract
- 1½ cups flour
- ½   teaspoon baking powder
- ½   teaspoon baking soda
- 2   9-ounce bags mini peanut butter cups
     mini muffin pans
     mini muffin papers

. . . .

Combine butter, peanut butter, sugar, brown sugar, egg, and vanilla extract. Mix well.

Add the flour, baking powder and baking soda and blend well.

Spray mini muffin tins with non-stick cooking spray. Take a teaspoonful of dough and shape it in a ball. Press lightly into muffin tins. Bake for 10 – 12 minutes in a preheated 350 degree oven until light brown. Remove from oven and press 1 mini peanut butter cup into the middle of each muffin. Cool in the refrigerator and then remove from tins. Place in paper cups.

Freezes well.

P.S. You'll have about 10 mini peanut butter cups left over. I freeze them and enjoy them when I crave something sweet.

You can also use sugar-free peanut butter cups

PIZZA COOKIE

The recipe looks like its name. Children can't believe it's a cookie and adults can't wait to eat it.

YIELD: 1 LARGE COOKIE   PREHEAT OVEN TO 350 DEGREES

Crust:
- 1 cup butter
- ½ cup sugar
- ½ cup brown sugar
- 1 egg
- 1 teaspoon vanilla extract
- 1¾ cup flour

Topping:
- 1½ cup peanuts
- 1½ cup mini marshmallows
- 16 ounces chocolate chips
- 25 glazed baking cherries (I use S & W Red Glace Cherries)
- 1 14-inch pizza pan sprayed with a non-stick cooking spray

. . . .

Mix butter, sugar, and brown sugar until fluffy. Add egg and vanilla extract and beat well on low speed. Then slowly add flour and blend well.

Spread dough onto pizza pan and bake in a preheated 350 degree oven for 12 to 15 minutes until golden. Top cookie dough with nuts, marshmallows, chocolate chips and cherries to look like a pizza (cheese, meat & sausage). Return to the oven until marshmallows melt. Cool slightly and cut with a pizza cutter into wedges or rectangles.

P.S. Alternative ways to use pizza dough, see the following recipe:
Pizza Fruit Delight

Freezes well.

LEMON MERINGUE COOKIES

This recipe can't be frozen, but it's a great treat and can be made the day before you need them.

YIELD: 20 COOKIES   PREHEAT OVEN TO 350 DEGREES

- 2 **egg whites**
- ⅔ **cup sugar**
- 1 **teaspoon vanilla extract**
- ⅛ **teaspoon cinnamon, optional**
- ½ **cup chopped pecans or walnuts**
- 6 **ounces chocolate chips**

. . . .

Beat egg whites on high speed until stiff. Gradually add sugar. Mix in all the remaining ingredients.

Line cookie sheets with aluminum foil and then spray with non-stick cooking spray (or use parchment paper). Drop dough by teaspoonfuls onto prepared sheets.

Place in a preheated 350 degree oven and immediately TURN OFF HEAT. Keep oven door closed and let cookies sit in the oven at least 8 hours. **

*** I make these cookies at night, before I go to bed.*
They are ready to eat the next morning!

GLAZED ALMOND LOVERS COOKIES

- 1 cup butter
- ¾ cup sugar
- 1 teaspoon almond extract
- 2 cups flour
- ½ teaspoon baking powder

Glaze:
- 1½ cups confectioners sugar
- 1 teaspoon almond extract
- 4-5 teaspoons water
- 8 ounces sliced almonds

Line a cookie sheet with parchment paper. Spray the paper with non-stick cooking spray.

In an electric mixer, cream the butter and sugar together. Add 1 teaspoon almond extract. Then add the flour and baking powder. Form dough into small balls. Press the balls down on prepared cookie sheets. Bake in a preheated 350 degree oven for 7-9 minutes. Cool.

Mix together the confectioners sugar, 1 teaspoon almond extract and water. Spread glaze on the cooled cookies. Then dip in a plate of sliced almonds. Let the glaze harden and enjoy.

Freezes well.

OATMEAL CARAMEL COOKIES

YIELD: 3 DOZEN COOKIES

PREHEAT OVEN TO 350 DEGREES

Cookie Mixture:
- 1 cup all purpose flour
- 1 teaspoon baking soda
- 1 cup uncooked oatmeal
- ¾ cup brown sugar
- ¾ cup butter, melted

Topping:
- 32 caramels, melted
- 5 tablespoons evaporated milk
- 1 cup chocolate chips
- ½ cup chopped pecans
- ¾ cup caramel ice cream topping
- 3 tablespoons flour

Cookie Mixture: Combine flour, baking soda, oatmeal, brown sugar and melted butter. Press ½ of mixture into a 9 x 13 pan sprayed with non-stick cooking spray. Bake in a preheated 350 degree oven for 10 minutes.

Topping: Melt caramel candies in evaporated milk. Stir constantly to prevent burning. Sprinkle chocolate chips, nuts and melted caramels over cookie base. Mix caramel ice cream topping with flour and pour over chocolate chip mixture. Spread to cover. Top with rest of cookie mixture and press down slightly.

Return to oven and bake an additional 15-20 minutes. Cool completely before cutting into squares.

This recipe freezes well.

FROSTED CASHEW TOPPED COOKIES

These cookies look as good as they taste.

YIELD: 50 COOKIES   PREHEAT OVEN TO 350 DEGREES

Cookie Mixture:
- 1 cup firmly packed brown sugar
- ½ cup butter
- ½ teaspoon vanilla extract
- 1 egg
- 2 cups all purpose flour
- ¾ teaspoon baking powder
- ¾ teaspoon baking soda
- ⅓ cup sour cream
- ¾ cup chopped cashew nuts

Frosting:
- ½ cup butter
- 2 cups confectioners sugar
- 3 tablespoons half and half
- ½ teaspoon vanilla extract
- 2 6-ounce bags whole cashew nuts for garnish

. . . .

Cookie Mixture: In a large bowl, beat butter and sugar until light and fluffy. Add vanilla extract and egg; beat well. Add flour, baking powder, baking soda and sour cream. Mix well. Add chopped nuts. Blend.

Spray cookie sheets with non-stick cooking spray. Drop by the spoonful onto prepared baking sheet and bake in a preheated 350 degree oven for 8-10 minutes. Remove cookies and cool.

Frosting: In a medium saucepan, lightly brown butter and remove from heat. Stir in confectioners sugar, half and half and vanilla extract. Beat until smooth. Frost cooled cookies and top each with a cashew.

This recipe freezes well.

GRANDMA ESTHER'S RUGALAH

This recipe comes from Arlene's mother, Esther Michlin. She is the best baker. Everything from her kitchen is always delicious.

YIELD: 40-45 PIECES   PREHEAT OVEN TO 350 DEGREES

Dough:
- 4 cups all purpose flour, sifted
- 1 cup butter (2 sticks)
- 1 cup sour cream (8 ounces)
- 2 egg yolks (reserve whites)
- vegetable oil to oil your hands

Filling:
- ½ cup melted butter (1 stick)
- 2 teaspoons cinnamon
- 1 cup sugar
- 1½ cups chopped walnuts
- ½ cup white raisins

Topping:
- ¾ cup sugar
- 1 teaspoon cinnamon

. . . .

Dough: Cut butter into flour with a pastry cutter or 2 knives. Add rest of ingredients; mix well with a wooden spoon as much as you can. Lightly oil your hands and continue to mix dough until you can form a ball. (After cutting in butter, the last steps can be done in a heavy-duty mixer.)

Divide into 4 balls. Wrap each in wax paper. Refrigerate about 1 hour.

Cover reserved egg whites and refrigerate.

Remove dough from refrigerator and let soften. Roll dough out on lightly floured board to form a circle if you wish to make crescents, or into a large rectangle if you want the rugalah in the form of strudel. Dough should be thin.

Filling: Brush dough with melted butter. Mix cinnamon, sugar, nuts and raisins together. Sprinkle over melted butter.

cont.

GRANDMA ESTHER'S RUGALAH, cont.

Cut dough into 12-16 wedges. Roll up into crescents with point tucked under or roll up jelly-roll fashion like strudel, fold ends under and cut in 1 inch slices. Place on ungreased cookie sheets. Brush with lightly beaten egg whites.

Topping: Mix sugar and cinnamon and sprinkle on rolled up dough.

Bake 20 to 25 minutes or until brown in a preheated 350 degree oven.

HAPPY MEMORY HOLIDAY COOKIES

When I think of my childhood, these cookies always come to mind. My grand-children love to make these with me. You don't have to wait for the holidays to make them.

PREHEAT OVEN TO 350 DEGREES

½ cup butter
1 cup sugar
1 egg, beaten well
1 teaspoon vanilla extract
1 tablespoon milk
2 cups flour
1½ teaspoons baking powder
lots of colored sugar and sprinkles

In an electric mixer, cream the butter. Then gradually add the sugar. Add the beaten egg, vanilla and milk. Gradually add the flour and baking powder.

Chill the dough in the refrigerator until you can handle it, about 2 hours. Flour a flat source and roll out the dough to about ½ inch. Use any cookie cutter you like and form cookies. Cover the cookies with colored sprinkles. Bake on a cookie sheet lined with parchment paper or sprayed with non-stick cooking spray. Bake in a preheated 350 degree oven for 12 minutes. Make sure to watch the cookies to prevent burning.

Freezes well.

ZELLA'S COOKIES

These cookies were given to me by the wonderful lady who originally typed up all my recipes for the book. Thanks Zella!

YIELD: 60 TO 70 COOKIES   PREHEAT OVEN TO 375 DEGREES

2½	cups flour
½	teaspoon salt
1	teaspoon baking soda
1	teaspoon baking powder
1	cup butter
1	cup brown sugar, packed
1	cup white sugar
2	eggs
2	teaspoons vanilla extract
2	cups oatmeal, pulverized
14	ounces chocolate chips
1½	cups chopped nuts (walnuts or pecans)

Sift flour, salt, baking soda and baking powder.

Cream butter and sugars. Add eggs and vanilla extract.

Add sifted ingredients, then oatmeal, chocolate chips and nuts.

Refrigerate 1 hour. Roll into walnut sized balls and place on ungreased cookie sheet, 2 inches apart.

Bake in preheated 375 degree oven for 8 minutes.

BRYN MAWR'S SECRET COOKIES

This cookie used to be made with the kitchen door closed, so no one could see how they were made at Bryn Mawr Country Club. But when the baker was replaced, the recipe got out and I was lucky enough to get it from my friend Terri D!

YIELD: 5 DOZEN COOKIES   PREHEAT OVEN TO 350 DEGREES

- 3 **cups firmly packed confectioners sugar**
- 7 **tablespoons cocoa**
- 2 **tablespoons flour**
- 3 **egg whites**
- 2 **cups chopped pecans**
-    **parchment Paper**

In a medium bowl, combine sugar, cocoa and flour. Add egg whites and beat on high speed for 1 minute. Turn speed down to low and stir in nuts.

Line cookie sheets with parchment paper. Drop scant teaspoon sized cookies onto pans. Bake in a preheated 350 degree oven for 15 minutes (Bake only 10 minutes for a chewier cookie). Cool on parchment before removing.

This recipe should NOT BE FROZEN. The cookies should be stored in an airtight container and are best eaten right out of the oven!

FLORENTINE COOKIES

YIELD: 30 SMALL COOKIES   PREHEAT OVEN TO 325 DEGREES

- 2 cups Quick Quaker Oats
- 1 tablespoon flour
- 2 cups sugar
- ½ teaspoon salt (optional)
- 1 cup melted butter (2 sticks)
- 2 eggs, beaten
- 1 teaspoon vanilla extract

Mix dry ingredients together. Pour hot butter over dry ingredients and stir until sugar is dissolved. Add eggs and vanilla extract. Stir well.

Line cookie sheet with aluminum foil. Drop by ½ teaspoons of dough 3 inches apart. Bake in a preheated 325 degree oven for 12 minutes. Cool for 10 minutes before removing from cookie sheet.

KRUNCHY KRISPIES

YIELD: 30 SQUARES

- 12 ounces butterscotch chips
- 1 cup creamy peanut butter (or cashew butter is terrific)
- 6 cups Rice Krispies cereal

In a double boiler, melt butterscotch chips and peanut butter. When melted, mix in Rice Krispies cereal. Pour onto a wax paper lined 9 x 13 x 2 pan sprayed with non-stick cooking spray (or line it with foil paper). Use wax paper to help pat mixture down into pan until it reaches the corners and is flat. Chill for 1 hour and then cut into squares.

TURTLE COOKIES

This recipe takes a little longer than most, but like the turtle, it's a real winner in the end!

YIELD: 30 COOKIES   PREHEAT OVEN TO 325 DEGREES

Cookie Dough:
- 10 tablespoons butter
- ⅔ cup brown sugar, firmly packed
- 1 egg
- 1 teaspoon vanilla extract
- 1¾ cup all purpose flour
- ½ teaspoon baking powder
- ½ teaspoon baking soda

Topping:
- 2 10 ounce packages of pecan halves
- 20 marshmallows cut in half
- 6 ounces semi sweet chocolate chips
- 1 12 ounce jar caramel sauce

. . . .

Cream butter and sugar until light and fluffy. Beat in egg and vanilla extract. Add flour, baking powder and baking soda. Mix until well blended.

For each "turtle", place 4 pecans on sprayed cookie sheets in an "X" shape. Take about a 1 inch ball of dough and press onto pecans. Bake about 10 minutes in a preheated 325 degree oven. Take out of oven when dough turns a light brown. Add a small amount of caramel sauce. On top of sauce press down a marshmallow half. Place back in oven until marshmallow melts. Take out of oven immediately and press marshmallow down with your hand once again (be careful not to burn yourself).

Melt the 6 ounces of chocolate chips. Dip turtle cookies into melted chocolate chips so that just the marshmallow is covered. Place cookies on wax paper until the chocolate hardens.

**The basic cookie dough is delicious just for sugar cookies

PEANUT MARSHMALLOW CHEWS

This recipe is an all-time favorite. After 25 years, both my new friends and old friends still request this recipe all the time.

YIELD: 36 PIECES   PREHEAT OVEN TO 350 DEGREES

Crust:
- 1½ cups all purpose flour
- ⅔ cup firmly packed brown sugar
- ½ teaspoon baking powder
- ¼ teaspoon salt
- ¼ teaspoon baking soda
- ½ cup butter
- 1 teaspoon vanilla extract
- 2 egg yolks
- 3 cups miniature marshmallows

Topping:
- ⅔ cup corn syrup
- ⅓ cup butter
- 2 teaspoons vanilla extract
- 12 ounces (2 cups) peanut butter chips
- 2 cups Rice Krispies cereal
- 2 cups salted peanuts (1 – 12 ounce can)

. . . .

Spray a 9 x 13 pan with non-stick cooking spray.

In a large bowl, combine all ingredients for the crust. Beat on a low speed until crumbly. Firmly press crust into prepared pan.

Bake in a preheated 350 degree oven for 12 to 15 minutes or until light golden brown. Immediately sprinkle with marshmallows and return to the oven for 1 to 2 minutes until marshmallows puff. Be sure to watch closely or the marshmallows will burn. Remove from oven and cool while preparing topping.

cont.

PEANUT MARSHMALLOW CHEWS, cont.

In a large saucepan, heat corn syrup, ⅓ cup butter, 2 teaspoons vanilla extract and peanut butter chips. Stir constantly until smooth. Remove from heat. Stir in cereal and nuts. Immediately spoon mixture onto marshmallows to cover.

Refrigerate until firm, then cut into bars.

This recipe can be frozen.

CINNAMON CARAMEL COOKIES

These cookies are quick, easy and delicious!

YIELD: 48 COOKIES   PREHEAT OVEN TO 350 DEGREES

- 24 cinnamon graham cracker squares
- ½   pound of butter
- 1   cup brown sugar, firmly packed
- 1½ cups chopped walnuts or pecans

Spray non-stick cooking spray on a large cookie sheet that has sides. Place all 24 cinnamon graham crackers on the pan. In a heavy saucepan, over low heat, melt butter and brown sugar. Bring to a boil and stir constantly for approximately 4-5 minutes or until it caramelizes. Pour the mixture evenly over cinnamon graham crackers. Sprinkle the top with chopped nuts.

Bake in a preheated 350 degree oven for 10 minutes. Cool for 10 minutes. Cut each square in half. There should be 2 rectangular cookies for each square. If I want very small cookies, I sometimes cut each cookies into 4 pieces.

SHORT BREAD COOKIES

   2 **cups sifted flour**
   ⅓ **cup corn starch**
   ½ **cup sugar**
   ½ **pound butter, softened**
   ½ **teaspoon vanilla extract**
   3½ **ounces ground walnuts**

Mix all of the ingredients together. Flour both your rolling pin and the surface where you'll be rolling out the dough to prevent it from sticking. I use a heart shaped cookie cutter, but any simple shape will do.

Spray cookie sheets with non-stick cooking spray. Bake in a preheated 350 degree oven for 14-20 minutes, until light brown.

P.S. When I'm very lazy I put all the batter on a jelly roll pan and pat down. I bake it 25 minutes until light brown and then cut into squares.

DEEP CHOCOLATE FUDGE DROPS

YIELD: 30 COOKIES

1	cup semi-sweet chocolate chips
1	cup butterscotch pieces or chips
1¼	cups Quaker Natural Granola
1	cup peanuts, chopped

. . . .

Melt chocolate and butterscotch chips in the top of a double boiler. Remove from the heat and stir in cereal and nuts.

Drop by teaspoons on wax paper lined pans. Chill in refrigerator until firm.

JAIME AND ABBY'S
PEANUT BUTTER COOKIES

Arlene's daughter Jaime and her friend, Abby created this recipe when they were pre-teens. These cookies are so easy that even little kids love to make them by themselves.

YIELD: 24 COOKIES   PREHEAT OVEN TO 350 DEGREES

- ¾ cup creamy peanut butter
- ½ cup butter
- 1¼ cups flour
- ½ cup sugar
- ½ cup brown sugar, firmly packed
- 1 egg
- 1 teaspoon baking soda
- 1 teaspoon baking powder
-    pinch of salt

Cream peanut butter and butter. Slowly add rest of the ingredients just until dough is firm.

Spray cookie sheet with non-stick cooking spray. Drop cookies by the spoonfuls. Lightly press each cookie with fork to create grooves. Bake in a preheated 350 degree oven for 10-12 minutes.

JELLY BUTTONS

I always double this recipe because its one of the fashion market favorites. People can't believe it's made with hard-boiled eggs.

YIELD: 40 COOKIES   PREHEAT OVEN TO 350 DEGREES

- ½ **pound butter**
- 2 **hard-boiled egg yolks**
- ¾ **cup sugar**
- 2¼ **cups flour**
  raspberry and apricot preserves (or any other flavor preserve)

Cream together butter, egg yolks and sugar. Add flour on low speed. Using your hand, roll dough into a cylinder-like form. Divide dough into 4 equal parts. Cut into ½ inch pieces and indent each to look like a thumb was stuck in the middle. Fill the indentation with the preserves.

Place on a cookie sheet sprayed with non-stick cooking spray and bake 12 minutes in a preheated 350 degree oven or until light brown.

INCREDIBLE CHOCOLATE CHIPS COOKIES

These cookies are huge! They are delicious right out of the oven or eaten frozen just out of the freezer.

YIELD: 40 COOKIES   PREHEAT OVEN TO 350 DEGREES

- ½ cup butter, softened
- 1½ cups butter flavored Crisco
- 1½ cups brown sugar
- 1 cup sugar
- 4 eggs
- 1 teaspoon vanilla extract
- 3½ cups flour
- 2 teaspoons baking powder
- 2 teaspoons baking soda
- 1½ cups regular oatmeal
- 16 ounces chocolate chips (chocolate chunks may replace chips)
  nuts (optional)

. . . .

Beat butter, Crisco, brown sugar, and sugar until fluffy, add eggs and vanilla extract and continue beating until creamy. Combine all dry ingredients and add to creamed mixture. Mix in chips and nuts.

Drop by the tablespoon onto cookie sheets sprayed with non-stick cooking spray. Leave room because they expand. Bake 10-12 minutes in a preheated 350 degree oven. Let cool a few minutes before removing from cookie sheet.

These cookies freeze well.

/COCONUT WALNUT CHUNK COOKIES

If you love coconut, then this recipe is for you.

PREHEAT OVEN TO 350 DEGREES

1 **cup butter**
1 **cup brown sugar**
1 **cup sugar**
2 **eggs**
1½ **teaspoon vanilla extract**
2¼ **cups flour**
½ **teaspoon salt**
1 **teaspoon baking soda**
2 **cups chocolate chunks**
2 **cups walnuts**
2 **cups shredded coconut**

In an electric mixer, cream together the butter, sugars, eggs and vanilla. Slowly add the flour, salt and baking soda. Mix in the chocolate, walnuts and coconut.

Form the mixture into balls. Use a teaspoon for small cookies. Use a tablespoon for large cookies. Place the balls onto cookie sheets sprayed with non-stick cooking spray or covered in parchment paper.

Bake in a preheated 350 degree oven for about 10 minutes. Let cool.

P.S. You can substitute pecans or use no nuts at all.

For a less sweet taste, substitute ¾ cup brown sugar and ¾ cup white sugar.

/CHOCOLATE BAR SURPRISE

The surprise is you don't know the chocolate is inside. I used to use a cookie shooter for this recipe. This is easier.

PREHEAT OVEN TO 350 DEGREES

1	**cup butter**
¾	**cup sugar**
1	**egg**
2	**teaspoon vanilla extract**
2½	**cups flour**
½	**teaspoon salt**
4-5	**1.45 ounce bars Hershey bars**
	confectioners sugar, for garnish

Spray a 9 x 13 pan with non-stick cooking spray.

Mix butter and sugar together. Add the egg, vanilla, salt and flour. Blend well. Press **half** of the dough into the prepared pan. Place chocolate bars over the dough (enough to cover) then cover with the rest of the dough.

Use the back of a fork to make ridges (optional). Bake for 25-35 minutes in a pre-heated 350 degree oven. Cut into small squares while still warm. Sprinkle with confectioners sugar if desired.

Freezes well.

MELTING MOUTHFULS

¾ cup butter
1 teaspoon vanilla extract
1 cup flour
½ cup sugar
¼ cup corn starch
    variety of colored sugars or sprinkles

Cream together butter and vanilla extract. Add flour, sugar and corn starch. Break off pieces of dough and roll into little balls. Take balls and roll them into colored sugar.

Place on a cookie sheet with non-stick cooking spray. Bake in a preheated 325 degree oven for 10 minutes. Cool on a wire rack.

WORLD'S BEST COCONUT MACAROONS

I make these for all holiday gatherings. People can't believe they didn't come from a bakery.

YIELD: 20 MACAROONS   PREHEAT OVEN TO 325 DEGREES

- 1 tablespoon + 2 teaspoons butter, melted
- 4 cups shredded coconut
- ¾ cup sweet condensed milk
- 1 egg, beaten slightly
- ¼ teaspoon vanilla extract
- 1 ounce melted chocolate for chocolate macaroons (optional)

Mix all ingredients together in a large bowl with a large spoon. Drop by the spoonfuls onto a cookie sheet sprayed with non-stick cooking spray.

Bake in a preheated 325 degree oven for approximately 20 minutes or until brown. Remove from oven immediately and cool.

P.S. If you want chocolate flavored macaroons, melt one ounce of chocolate and add to the batter -or- melt chocolate chips (or another type of dipping chocolate), dip the baked macaroons and place on a baking rack until chocolate hardens.

ANNIE'S OATMEAL CHOCOLATE CHIP COOKIES

YIELD: 48 COOKIES   PREHEAT OVEN TO 375 DEGREES

Cream:
- 2 cups corn oil margarine (room temperature)
- 2 cups sugar
- 2 cups brown sugar

Add:
- 4 eggs (room temperature)
- 2 teaspoons vanilla extract

Mix in:
- 4 cups flour
- 4¼ cups oatmeal – pulverized in processor
- 1 teaspoons salt
- 2 teaspoons baking powder
- 2 teaspoons baking soda

Add to above mixture:
- 24 ounces chocolate chips
- 1 8 ounce plain Hershey Bar – finely grated in processor
- 6 ounces chopped nuts, any kind (optional)

....

Roll dough to size of golf balls. Place on ungreased cookie sheets, 2 inches apart. Balls may be flattened a little.

Bake in a preheated 375 degree oven for 10 to 12 minutes.

DON'T OVER-BAKE! DO NOT LET COOKIES TURN BROWN IN OVEN!

Let cool on cookie sheet for 3-5 minutes and then cool on rack.

BLACK BOTTOM MUFFINS

My friend Barbara Adler gave me this recipe for our fashion market. It's always a hit!

YIELD: 4 DOZEN   PREHEAT OVEN TO 350 DEGREES

Bottom:
- 1½ cups flour, sifted
- 1 cup sugar
- ¼ cup cocoa
- 1 teaspoon baking soda
- ½ teaspoon salt
- 1 cup water
- ⅓ cup oil
- 1 tablespoon vinegar
- 1 teaspoon vanilla extract

Filling:
- 1 8 ounce cream cheese
- 1 egg
- ⅓ cup sugar
- pinch of salt (optional)
- 1 cup chocolate chips

. . . .

To prepare the "bottom", pour sifted flour into a mixing bowl. Add sugar, cocoa, baking soda and salt. Mix well. Add water, oil, vinegar and vanilla extract and beat until well blended. Set aside.

To prepare the "filling", beat cream cheese well and then add egg, sugar and salt. Add chocolate chips and stir until blended.

Spray mini-muffin tins with non-stick cooking spray or line each with a paper cup. Fill ⅔ of cup with "bottom" mixture and top with "filling" mixture (approximately ½ teaspoon).

Bake in a preheated 350 degree oven for 20 minutes. Test for doneness with a toothpick.

These muffins freeze well.

WHITE CHOCOLATE CHUNK COOKIES

YIELD: ABOUT 50 COOKIES   PREHEAT OVEN TO 350 DEGREES

2¼ cups all purpose flour
⅔ cup cocoa (I use Hershey's. but any brand will do)
1 teaspoon baking soda
½ teaspoon salt (optional)
1⅓ cups butter
1 cup sugar
⅔ cup firmly packed brown sugar
2 teaspoons vanilla extract
2 eggs
1½ cups white chocolate chips

Use non-stick cooking spray on baking sheets.

In a small bowl, combine flour, cocoa, baking soda and salt; set aside. In a large bowl combine butter, sugars and vanilla extract and beat well. Add eggs, one at a time, beating well after each addition. Gradually add flour mixture. Slowly beat in white chocolate chips. Drop by rounded teaspoons onto prepared cookie sheets.

Bake in a preheated 350 degree oven for 8 to 10 minutes. Cool 4 minutes and remove from cookie sheet.

Freezes well.

MELT IN YOUR MOUTH HAMENTASCHEN

YIELD: 20   PREHEAT OVEN TO 350 DEGREES

Dough:
- ½   cup butter
- 1   cup sugar
- 1   egg, beaten
- 2   tablespoons orange juice
- 1   teaspoon vanilla extract
- 2½   cups pre-sifted flour
- 2   teaspoons baking powder

Filling:

Preserves: any flavor your family would like. I use apricot, raspberry and blueberry. You can substitute chocolate chip, or prune, poppy seed or almond filling.

. . . .

Cream butter and sugar, Add beaten egg. Blend in orange juice and vanilla extract. Add flour and baking powder and mix well. Put dough in refrigerator for at least 3 hours.

Flour a flat surface and roll dough out. Use a circle cookie cutter to cut out the shapes. Add filling to each circle and fold into 3 cornered cookie. Pinch corner to hold shape. This will make mini cookies. Use a glass or jar top to increase size.

Place on a cookie sheet sprayed with non-stick cooking spray. Bake in a preheated 350 degree oven for 20 minutes or until light brown.

Freezes well.

CRUNCHY POPPY SEED COOKIES

YIELD: 5 DOZEN COOKIES   PREHEAT OVEN TO 350 DEGREES

- ½   **pound butter**
- 1½   **cups confectioners sugar**
- 2   **eggs**
- 3   **cups flour**
- 2   **teaspoons vanilla extract**
- 4   **tablespoons poppy seeds**

Cream butter and sugar. Add the eggs and blend well. Mix in the flour. Add vanilla extract and poppy seeds.

Roll the dough into small balls and place on a sprayed cookie sheet. Flatten each ball with a fork.

Bake in a preheated 350 degree oven for 15 minutes or until light brown.

Freezes well.

ALMOND COOKIES

  1   **8 ounce can of almond paste**
1¼   **cups sugar**
  2   **egg whites**

In a medium sized mixing bowl cut almond paste into small pieces. Beat in sugar and egg whites.

Grease cookie sheets and drop cookies in ½ teaspoon amounts approximately a ½ inch apart. Bake in a preheated 325 degree oven for 25-30 minutes until light brown and dry. Cool well before storing or freezing.

GRANDMA JEAN'S BUTTER CRESCENTS

This is my mother's Regina Jawer's recipe and my daughter Lizie's favorite. In fact, it is everyone's favorite. Its impossible to eat just one. I always double this recipe.

YIELD: 40 COOKIES   PREHEAT OVEN TO 350 DEGREES

- 1 cup butter
- 1 cup brown sugar
- 2 cups flour, sifted
- ¼ teaspoon salt (optional)
- 1 tablespoon water
- 1 teaspoon vanilla extract
- 2 cups finely chopped pecans
  confectioners sugar (for sprinkling on top of cooled cookies)

Cream butter. Add sugar, gradually. Blend well. Add sifted flour, salt, water and vanilla extract. Add chopped nuts and blend well. Break off small pieces of dough and form into small half moons.

Place on sprayed cookie sheets. Bake in a preheated 350 degree oven for 15 to 18 minutes. Cool and sprinkle with confectioners sugar.

Freezes well.

HERSHEY SQUARE SPRITZ COOKIES

YIELD: 32 COOKIES   PREHEAT OVEN TO 350 DEGREES

- 1   cup butter, softened
- ¾   cup sugar
- 3   large egg yolks
- 1   teaspoon vanilla extract
- 2¼   cups all purpose flour
- 5   Hershey Bars

Beat butter well. Gradually add sugar and beat about 5 minutes until light and fluffy. Add egg yolks and vanilla extract and beat well. Gradually add flour. The dough should be stiff.

Fill an electric cookie gun with about half the dough. Using ribbon disc, shoot out dough in strips on a sprayed cookie sheet. Break off little squares of Hershey chocolate bars and line them up vertically on the strips of dough. Fill cookie gun with remaining half of dough and shoot out strips to cover the Hershey Bar pieces.

Bake in a preheated 350 degree oven for 8 to 10 minutes. Cool the strips on the cookie sheet and then cut into squares.

CHOCOLATE DROP COOKIES

Karen Lee gave me this delicious recipe. She got it from her daughter's mother-in-law, Judy Guten. Both women are great bakers! Enjoy!

YIELD: 4 DOZEN COOKIES

4	squares unsweetened chocolate
1½	sticks butter
2	cups sugar
3	eggs
1	teaspoon vanilla
2½	cups flour
1	8-ounce container Cool Whip - do not defrost
6	squares semi-sweet chocolate

Microwave the unsweetened chocolate & butter until the butter is melted. Stir until the chocolate is completely melted. Add sugar, mix well. Blend in the eggs and vanilla. Then stir in the flour - do not overmix. Refrigerate for 1 hour or until the dough is easy to handle.

Shape into 1 inch balls - place 2 inches apart on lightly greased baking sheets (or parchment paper). Bake in a preheated 350 degree oven for 8 minutes or until set. Do not overbake. Cool Completely.

Put Cool Whip and chocolate in a microwave-safe bowl. Microwave for 30 seconds and repeat as needed until the chocolate is melted. Let stand 15 minutes to thicken. Spread over the cookies or dip them in the Cool Whip mix.

Let stand until firm.

HEAVENLY HASH

My grandchildren always request this recipe, but my daughter-in-law, Hadas begs me not to make the recipe because she can't stop eating them.

- 1½ 12 ounce packages of milk chocolate chips
- 6 ounces semi sweet chocolate chips
- 1 12 ounce jar crunchy peanut butter
- 6 ounces mini marshmallows

In an uncovered double boiler, melt the chocolate chips and peanut butter. Stir until smooth and melted. Add the mini marshmallows and stir to coat. Pour into a 9 x 13 pan sprayed with non-stick cooking spray.

Chill and cut into squares.

I put them into mini paper cups before freezing or serving.

CHOCOLATE BUTTONS

YIELD:48 COOKIES   PREHEAT OVEN TO 300 DEGREES

- ¼ cup butter
- 4 ounces (4 squares) unsweetened chocolate or 4 pre-melted packets unsweetened or baking chocolate
- 2 cups all purpose flour
- 2 cups sugar
- 2 teaspoons baking powder
- 3 eggs
- ½ cup chopped walnuts
  confectioners sugar

In a sauce pan, melt butter and chocolate over low heat. Stir constantly. Remove from heat and cool slightly. In a blender mix flour, sugar, baking powder and eggs. Add chocolate mixture on low speed. Add chopped walnuts and stir just until blended.

Chill dough in the refrigerator for 30 minutes. Break off small pieces of dough and shape into 1 inch balls. Roll in confectioners sugar and coat heavily. Place balls 2 inches apart on a sprayed or greased cookie sheet. Bake 15 to 18 minutes in a preheated 300 degree oven or until edges are light brown. Immediately remove from cookie sheet.

Freezes well.

MERINGUE RUGALAH

Dough:
- 4 cups flour
- ½ pound butter
- ¼ ounce dry yeast (1 package)
- 3 egg yolks, slightly beaten (reserve whites)
- ½ cup sour cream
- 1 teaspoon vanilla extract
  confectioners sugar for dusting

Filling:
- 3 egg whites
- 1 cup sugar
- 1 teaspoon vanilla extract
- 1 cup chopped walnuts

Cut butter into flour with pastry cutter. Sprinkle yeast into butter/flour mixture. Mix rest of ingredients together to form dough. Dough may be crumbly. Divide into 4 balls. Wrap in wax paper and refrigerate over-night or place in freezer for 1 hour. Cover reserved egg whites and refrigerate.

Dust board with confectioners sugar. Roll out each piece and cut in two (8 pieces total) Roll into thin, large rounds.

Prepare filling by beating egg whites until small peaks begin to form. Slowly add sugar and vanilla extract. Continue beating until stiff, but not dry. Stir in walnuts. Spread filling over dough.

Cut into small or large wedges. Roll up from large side to small point. Tuck point under. Place on greased cookie sheets.

Bake 15 to 20 minutes in a preheated 400 degree oven.

Cool on racks.

SNICKER DOODLE

Great with coffee or a cup of tea. This old fashioned cookie is a modern-day treat!

YIELD: 48 COOKIES   PREHEAT OVEN TO 350 DEGREES

- 1½ cups sugar
- ½ cup butter
- 2 eggs
- 1 teaspoon vanilla extract
- 2¾ cups all purpose flour
- 1 teaspoon cream of tartar
- ½ teaspoon baking soda

Topping:
- 2 tablespoons sugar
- 2 teaspoons cinnamon

Mix above together (add more if needed for topping)

. . . .

In a large bowl cream sugar and butter. Add eggs and vanilla extract and mix well. Add flour, cream of tartar and baking soda. Mix until dough forms.

Break off small pieces of dough and shape into 1 inch balls. Roll in the sugar and cinnamon mixture. Place about 2 inches apart on greased or sprayed cookie sheet. In a preheated 350 degree oven, bake 8 to 10 minutes or until light brown. Immediately remove from cookie sheet.

Freezes well.

BROWNIE DROP COOKIES

YIELD: 24 COOKIES   PREHEAT OVEN TO 350 DEGREES

- 2 **bars German sweet chocolate**
- 1 **tablespoon butter**
- 2 **eggs**
- ¾ **cup sugar**
- ¼ **cup sifted flour**
- ¼ **teaspoon baking powder**
- ¼ **teaspoon cinnamon**
- ½ **teaspoon vanilla extract**
- ¾ **cup chopped nuts**

Melt chocolate and butter in a double boiler. Stir and set aside to cool.

In a separate bowl, beat eggs until foamy Add sugar, 2 tablespoons at a time. Beat until thickened, approximately 5 minutes. Blend in cooled chocolate. Add flour, baking powder and cinnamon. Stir in vanilla extract and nuts.

Drop onto a greased cookie sheet and bake in a preheated 350 degree oven for 8-10 minutes.

These cookies freeze well.

CHOCOLATE PECAN CLUSTERS

YIELD: 24 COOKIES   PREHEAT OVEN TO 350 DEGREES

- 2 squares unsweetened chocolate, melted
- ½ cup butter
- 1 cup sugar
- 2 eggs
- 2½ teaspoons vanilla extract
- 1 cup flour
- ½ teaspoon baking powder
- 1 package chopped pecans
- 1 package caramels
- 1-2 tablespoons milk

Melt chocolate. Set aside to cool.

Cream butter and sugar. Add eggs and blend well. Add vanilla extract and cooled chocolate. Slowly mix in the flour, baking powder and pecans. Mix well.

Drop dough by teaspoonful onto a greased cookie sheet. Bake in a 350 degree oven for 10 minutes. Cookies should be soft.

While cookies are cooling, melt the caramels in a double boiler. When they start to melt, add milk and stir often to prevent burning (adjust the amount of milk to make caramels spreading consistency). Frost cooled cookies with caramel mixture.

Freezes well.

CHOCOLATE CHEWS

YIELD: 25 COOKIES   PREHEAT OVEN TO 350 DEGREES

1   12 ounce package of chocolate chips
4   tablespoons butter
1   can Eagle Brand Sweet Condensed Milk
1   cup flour
1   cup chopped walnuts or pecans
1   teaspoon vanilla extract

Melt chips, butter and milk in top of double boiler. Remove from heat. In the same pot add the flour, nuts and vanilla extract. Mix well.

Drop by teaspoons on a cookie sheet sprayed with non-stick cooking spray. Bake in a preheated 350 degree oven for 7 minutes. Cool cookies on a wire rack.

MEXICAN WEDDING COOKIES

- ½ pound butter, softened
- 4 tablespoons confectioners sugar
- 2 cups sifted flour
- 2 cups pecans, chopped fine
- 2 teaspoons vanilla extract
   confectioners sugar

Mix all ingredients together. Roll dough into small balls and place on a sprayed cookie sheet.

Bake in a preheated 350 degree oven until light brown, 10-12 minutes. Cool and roll in confectioners sugar.

ELEGANT LACE COOKIES

- ½   cup melted butter
- ½   cup + 2 tablespoons sugar
- 1   cup + 2 tablespoons quick oatmeal
- 1   tablespoon flour
- 1   teaspoon baking powder
- 1   egg
- 4   tablespoons slivered almonds
-     chocolate for dipping (optional)

Mix all ingredients together. Drop by ½ teaspoon onto sprayed foil paper on cookie sheet. Batter tends to spread so leave plenty of room.

Bake in a preheated 350 degree oven for 10 minutes. Watch carefully so they don't burn. Cool 15 minutes on foil before removing from pan.

These cookies are also wonderful when you dip them in melted chocolate discs. This chocolate can be purchased in a craft store, gourmet cooking store or grocery store. Hold the cookie and dip on one side. I like to see what the cookies look like so I don't cover the whole thing. Put the cookies on wax paper until the chocolate hardens.

CHOCOLATE CHUNK MACADAMIA COOKIES

YIELD: 60 SMALL COOKIES   PREHEAT OVEN TO 350 DEGREES

- 2 cups all purpose flour
- 1 teaspoon baking soda
- ½ teaspoon salt
- 1 cup (2 sticks) butter
- ¾ brown sugar, packed
- ½ cup sugar
- 1 teaspoon vanilla extract
- 1 egg
- 12 ounces semi sweet chocolate chunks
- 8 ounces or 2 small jars of Macadamia nuts, chopped chocolate for dipping (optional)

....

Spray cookie sheets with non-stick cooking spray.

In a small bowl, mix flour, baking soda and salt. Set aside. In a large bowl, combine butter, both sugars and vanilla extract; mix well until creamy. Beat in egg and add flour mixture. Beat well. Stir in chocolate chunks and nuts. Drop by rounded teaspoons about 2 inches apart on the cookie sheet.

Bake in a preheat 350 degree oven for about 8 to 10 minutes. Cool 10 minutes and remove from the cookie sheet.

These cookies can be dipped in melted chocolate discs by holding ½ the cookie and dipping the rest.

For a change of taste, substitute the Macadamia nuts with pecans, walnuts or coconut.

Freezes well

COCOA-BROWNIE COOKIES

These cookies are chewy and delicious!

YIELD: 25-30 COOKIES   PREHEAT OVEN TO 350 DEGREES

- 3 **cups firmly packed brown sugar**
- 7 **tablespoons cocoa (I use Droste's)**
- 2 **tablespoons flour**
- 3 **egg whites**
- 2 **cups chopped pecans**
  parchment paper

In a mixer, combine sugar, cocoa and flour until well blended. Add egg whites and beat on high speed for one minute. Reduce speed to low and add nuts. Stir just until blended.

Line cookie sheets with parchment paper. Drop teaspoon-sized cookies onto pan allowing room for cookies to spread. Bake in a preheated 350 degree oven for 15 minutes. Cool on cookie sheets for 3 minutes before removing to wire racks to cool.

DO NOT FREEZE. Store in an airtight container or a zip-lock bag.

MINI PECAN TARTS

Over the past 25 years, I have often used cherry pie filling in place of the pecan filling. They would probably be great with other pie filling flavors. Watch the time as they bake. The crust should be a light golden brown. Oven temperatures may vary and can influence your bake-time. Enjoy!

YIELD: 60 TARTS   PREHEAT OVEN TO 350 DEGREES

Base:
- 1⅓ cups butter
- 8 ounces cream cheese
- 2⅔ cups flour

Filling:
- 2 large eggs
- 1½ cups brown sugar
- 2 teaspoons butter, melted
- 2 teaspoon vanilla extract
- 1 cup chopped pecans
- confectioners sugar

Let butter and cream cheese soften at room temperature for about 1 hour, then mix well. Add flour and mix until the dough is soft. Chill for 1 hour.

Break off small pieces of dough and press into sprayed mini tins. Use a utensil with a rounded top that's been dusted with flour to spread dough evenly in muffin tins. Bake for 10-12 minutes in a preheated 350 degree oven until dough puffs up.

While the base is baking, prepare the filling. In a mixer, beat eggs and add brown sugar, melted butter, vanilla extract and nuts. Mix well.

Fill the muffin tins ¾ full with filling and return to oven for 15 minutes. Reduce oven to 250 degrees and bake for an additional 20 minutes or until brown. Remove from oven, let cool and then dust with confectioners sugar.

Freezes well.

POTATO CHIPS COOKIES

Every time I tell someone that there are potato chips in these cookies, they can't believe it. They are crunchy and yummy! Today you have the option to use baked or fat-free chips.

YIELD: 50 COOKIES   PREHEAT OVEN TO 350 DEGREES

- 2 cups butter
- 1 cup sugar
- 1 cup crushed potato chips (I always use Jay's)
- 1 teaspoon vanilla extract
- 1 cup crushed almonds
- 1 tablespoon almond extract
- 3 cups flour
- confectioners sugar

Cream ingredients in order: butter, sugar, potato chips, vanilla extract, crushed almonds and almond extract. Beat in flour and combine well.

Place by spoonfuls on a sprayed cookie sheet.

Bake in a preheated 350 degree oven for 10 to 12 minutes. Don't let them get too brown. When cool, sprinkle with confectioners sugar.

This recipe freezes well.

CHOCOLATE BON BONS

PREHEAT OVEN TO 350 DEGREES

- 1 **cup butter**
- ½ **cup unsifted confectioners sugar**
- 1 **teaspoon vanilla extract**
- 2¼ **cups sifted flour**
- 1 **14 ounce bag Hershey's kisses**

Cream butter and sugar. Blend in vanilla extract and add flour. Mix until well blended. Break off small pieces of dough and wrap around each Hershey's kiss until well formed.

Spray cookie sheet with non-stick cookie spray. Place cookies fairly close together. Bake in a preheated 350 degree oven for 10-12 minutes. Sprinkle with confectioners sugar when cool.

P.S. For a change, substitute the Kisses with nuts, baking cherries or mini chocolate candy of your choice.

CHOCOLATE CHIP BUTTER COOKIES

This recipe has become the number 1 favorite! Now that there are so many nut allergies I have been baking this recipe without the nuts.

YIELD: 40 COOKIES   PREHEAT OVEN TO 350 DEGREES

- ½ **pound butter**
- ½ **pound margarine**
- 1 **teaspoon vanilla extract**
- 1 **cup brown sugar**
- 3 **cups flour**
- 1 **6 ounce package of chocolate chips**
- ¾ **cup chopped pecans (optional)**
- **confectioners sugar for sprinkling**

. . . .

Cream butter and margarine. Add vanilla extract and brown sugar. Mix well. Add flour, chips and nuts. Blend well. Form dough into balls** and place on cookie sheets sprayed with non-stick cooking spray. Space cookies about a ½ inch apart. Bake in a preheated 350 degree oven for 15-20 minutes until light brown. Remove from oven and cool for ten minutes. Then sprinkle with confectioners sugar.

**Recently, I have been using a little demitasse spoon to make the tiniest cookies. Everyone loves them because they are so tiny you can eat several.

CRISP BROWNIE COOKIES

YIELD: APPROX. 48 SMALL BROWNIES   PREHEAT OVEN TO 350 DEGREES

- ½ cup butter
- 1 square unsweetened chocolate
- 1 egg
- ¼ teaspoon vanilla extract
- ½ cup sugar
- ½ cup sifted flour
- ½ cup chopped nuts (walnuts or pecans)

In a small pan, melt butter and square of chocolate. Remove from heat and beat in egg, vanilla extract and sugar. Add sifted flour and spread in a jelly roll pan sprayed with non-stick cooking spray. The mixture will be thin. Sprinkle with nuts.

Bake in a preheated 350 degree oven for 15 minutes.

Cut into squares immediately. This cookie will crisp as it cools. Store in an airtight container or freeze.

THE BEST BROWNIES AND BARS

THE BEST BROWNIES AND BARS

BETTER THAN SEX BROWNIES

I use a package of fudge brownie mix. But you can use my FUDGY RICH BROWNIES recipe if you like everything from scratch. These brownies are 3 layers thick.

YIELD: 36 BROWNIES   PREHEAT OVEN TO 350 DEGREES

Bottom layer:
>   Brownie mix or **FUDGY RICH BROWNIES**

Filling:
>   ½   cup butter
>   2   cups confectioners sugar
>   1   teaspoon vanilla extract
>   2   tablespoons milk

Topping:
>   6   ounce package semi sweet chocolate chips
>   4   tablespoons butter

. . . .

Bottom layer: Bake the brownies in a 9 x 13 pan sprayed with non-stick cooking spray following the package instructions. Cool for at least 1 hour.

Filling: Cream butter and add confectioners sugar, milk and vanilla extract. Beat until smooth. Spread mixture over cooled brownie layer. Refrigerate for at least 1 hour until firm.

Topping: Melt chocolate chips and butter – cool until spreading consistency. Spread over chilled filling.

Refrigerate again until the chocolate hardens. Cut into bars.

This recipe freezes well!

FUDGY RICH BROWNIES

You can use this brownie recipe as a base for all recipes I've given you or just as a great tasting brownie! My friend Felice introduced me to this recipe.

YIELD: 24-32 BROWNIES   PREHEAT OVEN TO 350 DEGREES

- 1   package (8 squares) Baker's unsweetened Chocolate
- 1   cup butter
- 5   eggs
- 3   cups sugar
- 1   tablespoon vanilla extract
- 1½ cups unsifted – all purpose flour
     optional – nuts or M & M's

....

Melt chocolate and butter in a sauce pan on very low heat stirring constantly. Cool.

Meanwhile, beat eggs, sugar and vanilla extract in a large mixing bowl on high speed for 10 minutes. Blend in chocolate mixture on low speed. Add flour, beating just to blend. Fold in any optional ingredients or leave them plain.

Spread mixture into a 9 x 13 pan sprayed with non-stick cooking spray. Bake in a preheated 350 degree oven for 35 – 35 minutes. Every oven is different so watch carefully and DO NOT OVERBAKE!

Cool and cut into squares.

These brownies are very rich, so you may want to cut them into smaller pieces.

CARAMEL BROWNIES

I use a packaged brownie mix for this recipe. But, if you want to make the batter from scratch, use the **Fudgy Rich Brownies** *recipe.*

YIELD: 36 BROWNIES   PREHEAT OVEN TO 350 DEGREES

- 1   **package brownie mix**
- 1   **bag Kraft caramels**
- 2½ **ounces evaporated milk (a little less than ½ cup)**
- 6   **ounce package chocolate chips**

. . . .

In a double boiler melt caramels with evaporated milk. Stir constantly. Prepare brownies according to the directions on package.

Spray a 9 x 13 pan with non-stick cooking spray and pour in ½ of brownie batter. Bake in a preheated 350 degree oven for 6 minutes.

Take baked brownies out of the oven and sprinkle on chocolate chips. Cover chips with melted caramel mixture. Cover with remainder of brownie batter and return to oven for an additional 25 minutes.

Cool completely and then cut into squares.

Freezes well!

ROCKY ROAD BROWNIES

I use a packaged brownie mix for this recipe when I'm in a hurry. Otherwise, I use the recipe for **Fudgy Rich Brownies** *when I want to make everything from scratch.*

YIELD: 36 BROWNIES   PREHEAT OVEN TO 350 DEGREES

- 1   brownie recipe
- 3   cups mini marshmallows
- 2   squares unsweetened chocolate
- 4   tablespoons butter
- ½   cup sugar
- ½   teaspoon vanilla extract
- 4   tablespoons milk

. . . .

Bake brownies and let cool.

Sprinkle top of brownies with mini marshmallows and place in a preheated 350 degree oven for a minute – just to slightly brown the marshmallows. Remove from oven and cool.

Prepare frosting by melting chocolate with butter. Remove from heat and beat with sugar, vanilla extract and milk in a mixer until spreading consistency. Spread over the cooled marshmallows.

Let brownies cool completely before cutting. Chill in the refrigerator to speed up the cooling process.

AUNTIE CAROL'S
FUDGY WUDGY BROWNIES

Carol Connors is my late husband's cousin. She is a song writer in Los Angeles. One of her most famous lyrics is the theme from "Rocky". These brownies are worth fighting for!

PREHEAT OVEN TO 325 DEGREES

- 4 squares Baker's Unsweetened chocolate
- ½ cup butter
- 4 eggs
- 2 cups sugar
- 1 cup sifted flour
- 1 teaspoon vanilla extract
- 1 teaspoon coffee liqueur
- 1 cup walnuts, chopped
- 1 6 ounce bag chocolate chip morsels
- ¼ cup coconut
- ¼ cup small marshmallows

Melt unsweetened chocolate and butter in a double boiler. Set aside to cool slightly.

In a large bowl beat eggs. Gradually add sugar and beat well. Add flour, vanilla extract and liqueur. Add cooled chocolate mixture and blend well. Stir in nuts and chocolate chip morsels.

Spread in a 9 inch square pan that has been sprayed with non-stick cooking spray. Sprinkle coconut and marshmallows on top and bake in a preheated 325 oven for 25-30 minutes.

Remove from oven and cool thoroughly in pan. Cut into squares and dig in!

/DREAMY CREAMY PEANUT FUDGIES

I woke up at 3 am with this inspiration for a new brownie. Served it at a party i gave and everyone went crazy for it. No one ate just one. Next time i'll make two batches!

- 1 **box fudge brownie mix**
- ½ **cup butter**
- 2 **cups confectioners sugar**
- 1 **teaspoon vanilla extract**
- 2 **tablespoons milk -OR- water**
- 4 **tablespoons creamy peanut butter**
- 6 **ounces chocolate chips**
- 4 **tablespoons butter**
- ½ **cup chopped peanuts for garnish, optional**

Bake the fudge brownies in an 8" square pan according to the directions on the package. Let cool.

Whip together ½ cup butter, confectioners sugar, vanilla, milk and peanut butter until smooth. Spread on the top of the cooled brownies. Chill in the refrigerator.

Melt the chocolate chips with 4 tablespoons butter. Spread over the chilled peanut butter layer. Sprinkle with chopped peanuts.

For extra thick brownies, use my Fudge Brownie recipe and use a 9 x 13 pan.

GERMAN CARAMEL BROWNIES

YIELD: 36 BROWNIES   PREHEAT OVEN TO 350 DEGREES

- 1   14 ounce package caramels
- 1   5 ounce can of evaporated milk
- 1   package Pillsbury German Chocolate Cake mix
- ¾   cup butter melted
- 1   cup chopped nuts
- 1   cup chocolate chips

Melt caramels and ⅓ cup evaporated milk in a heavy pan. Set aside.

Spray 9 x 13 pan with non-stick cooking spray.

Mix cake mix, butter and nuts together. Add ⅓ cup of evaporated milk. Mix again. Pat ½ of this mixture into pan and bake in a preheated 350 degree oven for 6 minutes. Remove from oven and sprinkle chocolate chips on top and then pour melted caramel mixture over the chips. Take rest of cake mixture and spread over caramel.

Bake for an additional 15-18 minutes. Cool for 30 minutes and then cut into squares.

Freezes well.

PECAN BARS

One day when I was baking for my business, I couldn't decide if I should make pecan tarts or not. That's when I made up this new recipe.

YIELD: 36 BARS   PREHEAT OVEN TO 350 DEGREES

Crust:
- 1 cup butter
- ½ cup sugar
- 2 cups flour

Filling:
- 2 teaspoons melted butter
- 1½ cups brown sugar
- 2 large eggs
- 2 teaspoons vanilla extract
- 1 cup chopped pecans
- confectioners sugar, for garnish (optional)

....

Crust:

Cream butter and sugar. Slowly add flour and blend well. Pat crust into a 10 x 15 jelly-roll pan sprayed with non-stick cooking spray and bake for 15 minutes in a preheated 350 degree oven. Remove from oven.

Filling:

Mix melted butter with brown sugar. Add eggs, vanilla extract and blend well. Add chopped pecans and mix well.

Pour filling over crust and return to oven for 15 minutes or until top is golden. Cool and cut into squares. If desired, sprinkle confectioners sugar.

Freezes well.

HERSHEY CANDY BAR SQUARES

1   cup butter
1   cup brown sugar, packed
1   egg yolk
1   teaspoon vanilla extract
2   cups flour
¼   teaspoon salt (optional)

Topping:
6   Hershey Bars
½   cup chopped walnuts or pecans

. . . .

Cream butter and brown sugar until fluffy. Add egg yolk and vanilla extract. Slowly, beat in flour and salt until well blended.

Spray a jelly-roll pan with non-stick cooking spray. Spread dough to cover pan. Use hands to press dough towards corners and pat down evenly. Bake for 20 to 25 minutes in a preheated 350 degree oven until light, golden brown. Remove dough from oven and place candy bars on hot dough until chocolate is soft and melting. Then spread with a knife until all the dough is covered with melted chocolate. Sprinkle with nuts. Cut into squares while warm.

GLAZED LEMON BARS

YIELD: 36 BARS   PREHEAT OVEN TO 350 DEGREES

Crust:

- 2 cups all purpose flour
- ½ cup confectioners sugar
- 1 cup butter

Filling:

- 4 eggs, slightly beaten
- 2 cups sugar
- ¼ cup flour
- 1 teaspoon baking powder
- ¼ cup bottled lemon juice
- 2 teaspoons lemon extract (for more "zip", use 1 tablespoon of lemon extract)

Frosting:

- 1 cup confectioners sugar
- 2-3 tablespoons lemon juice (depending on how tart you like it)
- ¼ cup lemon rind

. . . .

Spray a 9 x 13 pan with non-stick cooking spray.

Crust:

In a large bowl combine flour. Confectioners sugar and butter at low speed until crumbly. Press into a 9 x 13 pan.

Bake in a preheated 350 degree oven for 20 minutes or until light brown.

Filling:

In a large bowl combine eggs, sugar, flour and baking powder. Blend well. Stir in lemon juice and lemon extract. Pour mixture over warm crust.

GLAZED LEMON BARS, cont.

Return to oven and bake about 25 minutes or until top is light golden brown. Cool completely.

Frosting:

In a small bowl combine confectioners sugar, lemon juice and rind. Blend until smooth. Spread over cooled layer. Refrigerate. Cut into bars.

LAST MINUTE BARS

This recipe works whenever I need a quick, good cookie bar

YIELD: 36 BARS   PREHEAT OVEN TO 350 DEGREES

CRUST:
- ½ cup butter
- 1½ cups graham cracker crumbs

TOPPING:
- 1 cup chocolate chips
- 3/4 cup butterscotch chips
- ¾ cup chopped pecans or walnuts
- 1 cup shredded coconut
- 1 14 ounce can Eagle Brand Condensed Milk

. . . .

CRUST: Melt butter in 9 x 13 pan in oven. Add graham cracker crumbs and mix well with a fork. Press mixture evenly down in pan to form a crust.

TOPPING: Sprinkle both chips over crust. Sprinkle nuts over chips. Sprinkle coconut over nuts. Slowly drizzle condensed milk evenly over all ingredients.

Bake in a preheated 350 degree oven for 25 minutes (coconut and milk should turn light brown).

Cool 30 minutes and then put in refrigerator to harden. Cut into 2x2 squares.

These bars freeze well.

CHEESECAKE SQUARES

PREHEAT OVEN TO 350 DEGREES

Crust:
- ¾ cup butter
- ⅓ cup packed light brown sugar
- ½ cup sugar
- 2 cups flour

Topping:
- 16 ounces cream cheese, room temperature
- ½ cup sugar
- 2 eggs
- 1 teaspoon vanilla extract

. . . .

Spray a 9 x 13 pan with non-stick cooking spray.

For the crust, beat together the butter and sugars. Add flour, one tablespoon at a time. Pat the crust into the prepared pan. Bake in a preheated 350 degree oven for 10-15 minutes or until semi-firm.

For the topping, beat together the cream cheese and sugar for about 2 minutes in an electric mixer. Add the 2 eggs and vanilla. Pour the mixture over the baked crust. Bake for 25 minutes in the preheated 350 degree oven. Cool and cut into squares.

Freezes well.

P.S. You can add blueberries, strawberries, raspberries, cherries, or chocolate chips on top. Get creative!

YUMMY RASPBERRY BARS

YIELD: 36 BARS   PREHEAT OVEN TO 350 DEGREES

Crust:

- 2 cups flour
- ½ cup sugar
- pinch of salt (optional)
- 1 cup butter
- 1 cup raspberry preserves

Topping:

- 1½ cups packed brown sugar
- 3 large eggs
- ½ teaspoon vanilla extract
- ½ cup chopped walnuts
- ¾ cups flaked coconut
- 4½ tablespoons flour
- ¾ teaspoon baking powder
- confectioners sugar (optional)

Beat the ingredients for the crust, minus the preserves, together until crumbly. A good method is to mix flour, sugar and salt. Cut up the frozen butter in 1 tablespoon portions. Put in food processor and turn on/off until crumbly. Pat dough mixture into sprayed jelly roll pan and bake until light brown for 15 to 18 minutes in a preheated 350 degree oven.

Cool crust about 15 minutes and spread 1 cup raspberry preserves over warm crust.

Topping:

On high speed, beat brown sugar, eggs and vanilla extract in a large mixing bowl for 2 to 4 minutes. The mixture should be fluffy. Add walnuts, coconut, flour and baking powder. Stir until batter is well blended. Spread topping over preserves.

YUMMY RASPBERRY BARS, cont.

Reduce the oven to 325 degrees and bake an additional 20-30 minutes until top is brown and center is firm. Cut warm bars in 1½ - 2 inch squares. To increase the number of bars, the squares can then be recut on a diagonal, to create triangle pieces.

Sprinkle with confectioners sugar (optional).

ESTHER'S STRUDEL

Esther Michlin is a fabulous baker. She used to watch her mother, Frieda Fisch make this strudel. It has an "old-world" flavor and texture. Well worth the time and effort!

YIELD: 40 PIECES   PREHEAT OVEN TO 350 DEGREES

Dough:
- 1 cup butter, softened
- 8 ounces sour cream
- 2¼ cups all purpose flour

Filling:
- 2 large jars apricot preserves (36 ounces)
- 2 cups chopped walnuts
- 2½ cups white raisins
- confectioners sugar

. . . .

Cream butter in mixer. Alternate adding small amounts of sour cream, then flour, until it becomes heavy to keep mixing. Add remaining flour with a spoon, or by hand. Dough will be sticky.

Divide into 4 parts and wrap each part in wax paper. Refrigerate overnight.

Remove dough from refrigerator and let soften.

Roll dough out on floured board. It should be as thin as possible and shaped into a rectangle. Spread generously with apricot preserves (not jelly), followed by a sprinkling chopped walnuts and white raisins. Tightly roll and fold ends under. Place all 4 rolls side by side on a large jelly roll pan which has been well greased.

Bake 1 hour in a preheated 350 degree oven until light golden brown. Cut while warm in 1 inch slices. Cool on pan. Stores well in tin cans. Freezes well.

Sprinkle with confectioners sugar before serving.

ZESTY LEMON BARS

A friend asked me what she could bake with fresh lemons she got off a tree. I gave her this recipe. She said it was a winner!

PREHEAT OVEN TO 350 DEGREES

Crust:
- 1 cup butter
- 2 cups flour
- ½ cup confectioners sugar

Topping:
- 4 eggs
- 2 cups sugar
- 4 tablespoons flour
- 1 teaspoon baking powder
- 4 tablespoons lemon juice (you can squeeze fresh lemons)
- 1 tablespoon lemon extract
- 1 tablespoon grated lemon rind (optional)
- confectioners sugar

. . . .

Crust:

Beat butter and add flour and sugar. Press into a sprayed jell roll pan. Bake for 15 minutes in a preheated 350 degree oven.

Topping:

On medium speed beat eggs and sugar. Add flour, baking powder, lemon juice, lemon extract, and lemon rind. Beat for 2 minutes and pour evenly over hot crust. Return to oven and bake for another 25 minutes. When cool, sprinkle with confectioners sugar and cut into squares.

SIX LAYER FRUITY STRUDEL

Dough:
- 2¾ cups flour
- 1 teaspoon baking powder
- 1 teaspoon baking soda
- 2 tablespoons water
- 6 eggs separated, reserve 2 of the egg whites
- ½ cup vegetable oil
- 2 orange rinds, grated
- 1 lemon rind, grated

Filling:
- 1 cup nuts, finely chopped
- 1 teaspoon cinnamon
- 1 cup sugar
- 1 cup white raisins
- 2 cups apricot preserves (optional – strawberry or blueberry)

. . . .

Mix dough ingredients together and divide into 6 balls. Roll out first ball to fit a 9 x 13 pan sprayed with non-stick cooking spray. Place on bottom.

To prepare filling, combine all ingredients except for preserves.

Sprinkle dough with filling and dot with preserves. Put second layer of dough on top and repeat process. Reserve a small amount of filling to use as a garnish.

Bake in a preheated 350 degree oven for 20 minutes.

Remove from oven and glaze with remaining egg whites that have been whipped. Sprinkle rest of sugar mixture on top. Bake 20 minutes more.

Cool 20 minutes and cut into squares.

MY MOTHER'S MANDEL BREAD

My mother, Regina Jawer, was always asked to bring this recipe whenever people invited her over.

YIELD: ABOUT 60 PIECES   PREHEAT OVEN TO 350 DEGREES

- 1 cup butter
- 1 cup sugar
- 4 eggs
- ⅛ teaspoon salt (optional)
- 1 teaspoon vanilla extract
- 4 cups flour, sifted
- 1 teaspoon baking powder
- 1 cup nuts, chopped – walnuts or pecans
- 1 teaspoon cinnamon

Cream butter and sugar. Add eggs, salt and vanilla extract. Add the sifted flour, baking powder and chopped nuts. Blend well.

Divide dough into 4 parts. Shape dough into long loaves on cookie sheets sprayed with non-stick cooking spray. Bake in a preheated 350 degree oven until light brown, about 30-35 minutes. Remove from oven and cut into ½ inch slices. Lay slice on side and put back in oven for a few more minutes to brown. Combine cinnamon and sugar. Sprinkle while warm.

Freezes well.

ICE CREAM ROLL UPS

Thanks, Lori Lavin!

YIELD: 48 PIECES   PREHEAT OVEN TO 350 DEGREES

Dough:
- 1   pint vanilla ice cream (I use Hagen Daz), softened*
- 1   pound margarine, softened
- 4   cups flour

Filling:
- 1   small jar apricot jam
- 1   small jar raspberry jam
- 1   box white raisins
- 1   3 ounce container cinnamon sugar
  confectioners sugar for decoration (optional)

· ·

In a mixer, beat ice cream, margarine and flour. Mix well and knead briefly. Chill overnight or several hours in a wax paper covered bowl. Divide dough into 8 balls. Roll out into rectangle forms on a lightly floured surface (flour the rolling pin because the dough is sticky). On the rolled out dough, spread a layer of jam (use only one flavor per roll). Cover jam with raisins and then sprinkle on a layer of cinnamon and sugar. Roll up like a jelly roll and tuck ends under.

Place on cookie sheets sprayed with non-stick cooking spray. Bake in a preheated 350 degree oven for 45 minutes. Cut while warm.

When cool, sprinkle with confectioners sugar.

The dough can be made ahead and frozen. The completed roll ups freeze well!

for those on a restricted diet, tofu can be substituted.

MY FAVORITE CAKES AND PIES

MY FAVORITE CAKES AND PIES

SO YOU WANT TO BAKE YOUR OWN PIE CRUST...

1½   cups sifted flour
½   teaspoon salt
½   cup shortening
4-5   tablespoons cold water

....

Sift flour and salt. Cut in shortening until crumbly. Sprinkle water over crumbs a little at a time and mix after each addition until dough can be formed into a ball.

Lightly flour a surface and roll out ball to size of pie plate. Fold dough in quarters and then place in center of plate. Unfold and gently pat to the form of the pan. Remove any excess on the edges.

For a double crust:
2   cups flour
1   teaspoon salt
⅔   cup shortening
5-7   tablespoons cold water

....

Divide dough into 2 balls and follow above directions

CREAM CHEESE FROSTING

    1   8 ounce package cream cheese, softened
 1½   cups confectioners sugar
    ½   cup heavy whipped cream or Cool Whip

Beat cream cheese until fluffy. Add the sugar and cream. Beat until smooth. Use on my Flourless Chocolate Cake recipe or any of your favorite cake recipes. Keep refrigerated.

CHOCOLATE CHIP PIE

My friend Margie gave me this recipe. This is a special dessert if you want to impress your company.

PREHEAT OVEN TO 325 DEGREES

2	eggs
½	cup flour
½	cup sugar
½	cup firmly packer brown sugar
1	cup butter, melted and cooled to room temperature
6	ounce package semi sweet chocolate chips
1	cups chopped walnuts
1	9 inch unbaked pie shell

In a large bowl beat eggs until foamy. Beat in flour, sugar and brown sugar until well blended. Blend in melted butter. Stir in chocolate chips and walnuts. Pour batter into a pie shell.

Bake 1 hour. Remove from oven and serve warm. This pie is delicious served with ice cream and whipped cream.

This pie freezes well.

MY BEST APPLE PIE

My parents used to bring me a bushel of apples every year from their trees. So what did I do? I baked apple pies to last the whole year. I like using Granny Smith apples.

PREHEAT OVEN TO 350 DEGREES

- 2   frozen or refrigerated pie shells
- 6   baking apples, peeled and sliced
- ¾   cup sugar
- 2   tablespoons all-purpose flour
- ½   teaspoon cinnamon dash nutmeg
- 2   tablespoons butter

Mix together the sliced apples, sugar, flour, cinnamon and nutmeg. Pour into a prepared pie shell. Dot top of apples with butter and cover with second pie shell. Pinch top and bottom of crusts together so they totally cover the pie. Make small slits on top of pastry to make sure the pie bakes thoroughly.

Bake in a preheated 350 degree oven for 1 hour or until crust is light brown.

P.S. This pie is delicious served warm with ice cream. When in season, peaches make a fabulous substitute.

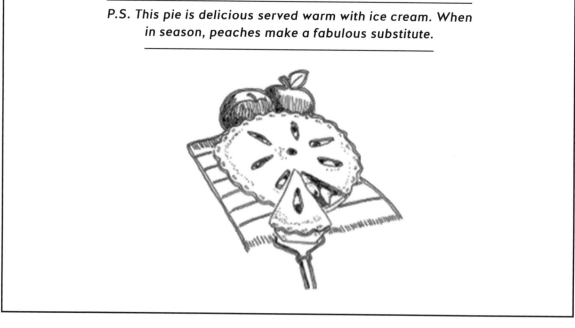

/APPLE CRISP

PREHEAT OVEN TO 350 DEGREES

4   Granny Smith apples, cut into chunks
¼   teaspoon cinnamon
⅛   teaspoon cloves
1   cup flour
½   cup brown sugar
¼   cup sugar
⅓   cup oats
½   cup butter

Spray an 8" square or 9" round pie pan with non-stick cooking spray.

Toss the apple chunks with cinnamon and cloves. Place the mixture in the bottom of a prepared pan.

Mix together the flour, sugars, oats and butter. Use your fingers to combine into a crumbly mixture. Top the apples with the crumb mixture.

Bake for 1 hour in a preheated 350 degree oven.

QUICK & EASY BANANA CREAM PIE

1 graham cracker crust
2 bananas
1 pint vanilla ice cream
1 cup milk
1 banana instant pudding

Slice bananas and cover the bottom of a graham cracker crust. Whip ice cream, milk and instant pudding together. Pour mixture over bananas and chill until set.

Serve and enjoy.

COCONUT CREAM LEMON CAKE

Cake:
- 1 Duncan Hines Yellow Cake Mix
- 1 cup sour cream
- 4 eggs
- ¾ cup vegetable oil
- 1 package lemon pudding

Frosting:
- 2 cups confectioners sugar
- ½ cup unsalted butter, softened
- 1 tablespoon lemon extract
- 1 tablespoon milk OR water
- 7 ounces shredded coconut, divided

Grease a bundt pan with non-stick cooking spray.

In a large bowl, mix all ingredients for the cake together. Bake as directed on the package, about one hour. Cool for one hour and invert on a plate.

For the frosting, beat the confectioners sugar, butter, lemon extract and water together until smooth. Add half of the coconut to the frosting and mix well. Spread the frosting on the cooled cake. Pat the frosting on the cake so it sticks about half way down the cake. Then sprinkle with the remaining coconut. You may need to use your hands to help pat down the coconut.

YUMMY COCONUT CREAM PIE

This pie works with a sugar substitute if you want to keep your sugar down.

Bake **1 pie shell** and let cool until ready to use.

PREHEAT OVEN TO 350 DEGREES

Filling:
- ¾ cup sugar
- 4 tablespoons cornstarch
- ¼ teaspoon salt
- 3 eggs separated
- 2 cups milk, scalded
- 1 tablespoon butter
- 1 teaspoon vanilla extract
- 2 cups shredded coconut

In a medium saucepan mix together ½ cup sugar, cornstarch and salt. Add egg yolks and mix in 2 tablespoons of scalded milk. Blend well. Add rest of milk and beat until smooth. Cook over low heat until thick. Beat in butter and vanilla extract. Remove from heat.

Take ¼ can of coconut and sprinkle some on bottom of pie crust. Add ¼ of coconut to batter and stir. Pour ½ batter into pie shell. Take another ¼ can of coconut and sprinkle on top of filling. Then add remainder of filling to pie shell, reserving balance of coconut for topping.   To prepare topping, whip egg whites and ¼ cup sugar together until they form peaks. Cover pie with meringue topping and sprinkle remaining coconut on top.

Bake in a preheated 350 degree oven for about 20 minutes or until meringue is browned. Watch to prevent burning.

CHOCOLATE PECAN PIE

This pie tastes great warm! As an extra treat, serve it with ice cream or whipped cream. Delish!

PREHEAT OVEN TO 350 DEGREES

1   unbaked pie shell
3   eggs
1   cup Karo light or dark corn syrup
1   package (4 ounces) Baker's German Sweet Chocolate or 4 squares semi sweet chocolate, melted and cooled
⅓   cup sugar
2   tablespoons butter, melted
1   teaspoon vanilla extract
1½ cups pecan halves

In a large bowl, mix eggs, corn syrup, melted and cooled chocolate, sugar, melted butter and vanilla extract. Stir until well blended. Fold in pecans.

Pour into pastry shell and bake in a preheated 350 degree oven for 50-60 minutes until set.

Freezes well!

PIZZA FRUIT DELIGHT

This recipe is great on a hot summer day. It looks cool and refreshing and tastes delicious.

PREHEAT OVEN TO 350 DEGREES

  1 14 inch pizza pan

Crust:

  1 cup butter
  ½ cup sugar
  ½ cup packed brown sugar
  1 egg
  1 teaspoon vanilla extract
1¾ cup flour

  1 8 ounce cream cheese, whipped in a mixer
  2 cans sliced peaches
  1 pint strawberries
20 green grapes
  1 pint blueberries
  1 8 ounces Cool Whip

To make crust: In a large bowl, beat butter, add sugar and brown sugar and beat until fluffy. Add egg and vanilla extract and beat well. Add flour on low speed and blend well. Spread the dough evenly onto a sprayed 14 inch pizza pan.

Bake crust in a preheated 350 degree oven for about 12 minutes until golden brown. When cool, lightly spread crust with whipped cream cheese. Pat dry sliced peaches and arrange on top of the cream cheese. Place grapes, sliced strawberries and blueberries on top. You can arrange the fruit in a wedge style to resemble a cut up pizza or just place to fill entire pizza. You do not have to use all the blueberries or all the strawberries.

PIZZA FRUIT DELIGHT, cont.

Dollop a little whipped topping for decoration. Cut and enjoy.

Pizza dough, without topping, may be frozen.

All other seasonal fresh fruits can be used. If using bananas, serve immediately because they turn brown.

JASON'S FAVORITE CHOCOLATE PISTACHIO CAKE

This is my son's favorite cake. I've been making it especially for him for at least 37 years!

PREHEAT OVEN TO 350 DEGREES

Mix together:
- 1   package white or yellow cake mix
- 4   eggs
- ¾   cup oil
- 1   cup sour cream
- 1   3.4 ounce box <u>instant</u> pistachio pudding
- 1   5½ ounce Hershey Chocolate Syrup
   confectioners sugar

Mix all ingredients except syrup, with an electric beater on medium. Pour ¾ of mixture into a greased or sprayed bundt pan. Add syrup to remaining batter. Mix well and pour on top of batter in bundt pan. Take a knife and run it through batter using a swirling motion. This will marbleize the batter.

Bake in a preheated 350 degree oven for 50-60 minutes. Check for doneness with a toothpick. Remove from oven and cool for 1 hour. Turn onto a plate and sprinkle with confectioners sugar.

LIZIE'S LEMON SURPRISE CAKE

My daughter Lizie makes this cake for me at market time. The surprise is that it's easy! This recipe comes from our friend Susie.

- 2 cans lemon custard (Thank You brand or other lemon pie filling)
- 2 packages lady fingers
- 1 8 ounce Cool Whip
- 1 pint fresh strawberries, sliced

Spray a 9 inch springform pan with non-stick cooking spray.

Place lady fingers on bottom of springform and stand them up next to each other to line inside border of pan. Pour 1 can of lemon custard on top of the lady fingers, then add ½ container of Cool Whip, sliced strawberries to cover Cool Whip and then add another layer of lady fingers. Repeat lemon and Cool Whip with strawberries being top layer.

Chill at least 2 hours. Unmold and serve.

Looks great and tastes fantastic!

SOUR CREAM COFFEE CAKE

This recipe was requested by the Chicago Sun Times.

PREHEAT OVEN TO 350 DEGREES

1	cup butter
2¼	cups sugar
2	eggs beaten
2	cups sour cream
1	tablespoon vanilla extract
2	cups all purpose flour
1	tablespoon baking powder
½	cup chopped pecans
2	teaspoons cinnamon

Cream together butter and 2 cups of sugar (reserving ¼ cup of sugar). Add eggs and blend well. Add sour cream and vanilla extract.

Sift flour and baking powder. Add to creamed mixture, beat until blended.
DO NOT OVER BEAT!

In a separate bowl mix ¼ cup sugar with pecans and cinnamon.

Spray bundt pan with non-stick cooking spray. Pour ½ of dough mixture into bundt pan. Sprinkle with ¾ of cinnamon, sugar and nut mixture. Reserve ¼ of sugar mixture to top of cake. Add remaining batter and top with sugar mixture.

Bake in a preheated 350 degree oven for 1 hour. Cool for 1 hour before unmolding.

This cake is incredibly moist and freezes well.

BAKED MERINGUE SPICED CAKE

PREHEAT OVEN TO 350 DEGREES

2⅔ cups cake flour
1 teaspoon ground cloves
1 teaspoon baking powder
1 teaspoon baking soda
1 teaspoon cinnamon
½ pound butter
2 cups brown sugar, packed
2 eggs + 2 egg yolks, beaten
1 cup sour milk (To make sour milk, add 1 tablespoon vinegar to regular milk. Let sit about 1 hour).

Meringue:
2 egg whites
1 cup brown sugar
½ cup chopped nuts

....

Sift flour, ground cloves, baking powder, baking soda and cinnamon 3 times. Set aside.

Cream butter and sugar until fluffy. Add beaten eggs and yolks. Beat thoroughly. Add sifted dry ingredients, alternating with milk.

Pour into a 9 x 13 pan sprayed with non-stick cooking spray.

To make meringue use a small, clean, dry bowl. Put in egg whites and beat on high speed. When foamy, slowly begin to add brown sugar and beat until peaks begin to form. Do not over process. Stir in nuts. Spread meringue on top of cake and bake in a preheated 350 degree oven for about 1 hour. Let cool before cutting.

/CINNAMON CAKE

I got this recipe from Joanne Savage. It is quick, easy, and so delicious!

PREHEAT OVEN TO 325 DEGREES

1 box yellow cake mix (without pudding)
See instructions on box for adding:
vegetable oil
water
eggs (plus one extra)

1 large box of Instant Vanilla pudding (approximately 6 ounces)
cinnamon & sugar mixture...either pre-made or 1/4 teaspoon cinnamon
to 1 cup sugar
(more cinnamon to taste)

Follow directions on box of yellow cake mix. Add water, oil and eggs...Add 1 additional egg (usually 4 total) and the pudding mix. Beat on medium for 2 minutes.

Spray a Bundt pan with non-stick cooking spray, including the sides and middle. Generously sprinkle with cinnamon sugar mixture.

Add 1/2 the batter. Sprinkle with a **thick** layer of cinnamon/sugar mixture. Add the rest of the batter.

See baking instructions on the box. Place in a preheated 325 degree oven for 45 minutes...check for doneness with a toothpick. The top will be light golden brown. Watch as ovens vary.

Let cool in pan for 10 -15 minutes. Then invert on a plate. The cake should slide out easily. Let cool and then slice.

Delicious!

JACKIE'S COFFEE CAKE

At market time, my friend Jackie makes this cake for me. It's a real treat!

PREHEAT OVEN TO 325 DEGREES

- ½ cup butter
- 1 cup sugar
- 2 eggs
- 2 cups flour
- 1 teaspoon baking soda
- 1 teaspoon baking powder
- ½ teaspoon salt
- 1 cup sour cream
- 1 teaspoon vanilla extract

Topping:
- ⅓ cup brown sugar
- ¼ cup sugar
- 1 teaspoon cinnamon

Cream butter until soft. Add sugar, and cream until light & fluffy. Add eggs one at a time and beat well. Sift together flour, baking soda, baking powder and salt and add to the creamed mixture. Stir in sour cream and vanilla extract. Mix well.

In a separate bowl, prepare topping by combining brown sugar, sugar and cinnamon.

Pour ½ batter into a 9 x 13 pan sprayed with non-stick cooking spray. Cover with ¾ topping mixture. Pour on the remaining batter and sprinkle on remaining topping.

Bake for 40 minutes in a preheated 325 degree oven. Let cook before cutting into squares.

This cake freezes well.

CHOCOLATEY RICH FLOURLESS CAKE

I make this recipe for many holidays. It is so delicious for any gathering of family and friends!

PREHEAT OVEN TO 325 DEGREES

- 7 ounces semi-sweet chocolate
- ¼ pound unsalted butter
- 7 eggs, separated
- 1 cup sugar
- 1 teaspoon vanilla extract
- ⅛ teaspoon cream of tartar
  Cool Whip, regular or chocolate

Spray a 9" spring form pan with non-stick cooking spray.

In a small saucepan melt the chocolate and butter at low heat until smooth.

In a large bowl, beat the egg yolks and ¾ cup sugar until light and fluffy, about 3 minutes. Slowly beat in the warm chocolate mixture and vanilla.

In another bowl, beat egg whites and cream of tartar until it peaks. Add remaining ¼ cup sugar, one tablespoon at a time. Continue beating until stiff. Fold egg whites carefully into chocolate mixture. Pour into the prepared spring form pan.

Bake 30 – 35 minutes in a preheated 325 oven. Let cool and remove ring. Refrigerate until firm or you can freeze.

Top with Cool Whip or whipped cream and enjoy.

BETTER THAN CHOCOLATE CAKE

PREHEAT OVEN TO 350 DEGREES

- 1 box yellow cake mix
- 1 3.4 ounce box instant vanilla pudding
- ½ cup vegetable oil
- ½ cup water
- 4 eggs (one at a time)
- 1 cup sour cream
- 1 bar grated German chocolate
- 1 6 ounce package chocolate chips
- 1 6 ounce package butterscotch chips
- ½ cup chopped pecans

On medium speed, combine cake mix, pudding, oil and water until blended. Add eggs, one at a time, and blend well. Add sour cream and mix again.

By hand, fold in grated German chocolate, chocolate chips, butterscotch chips and chopped pecans. Spray a bundt pan with non-stick cooking spray and pour in the batter.

Bake in a preheated 350 degree oven for 1 hour. Cool for 1 hour before removing from pan.

Freezes well.

CHOCOLATE CHIP CAKE

PREHEAT OVEN TO 350 DEGREES

¼ pound sweet butter
1 cup sugar
2 eggs
2 cups sifted cake flour
1 teaspoon baking powder
1 teaspoon baking soda
½ pint sour cream
1 teaspoon vanilla extract
6 ounces semi sweet chocolate chips
  confectioners sugar

Spray a bundt pan with non-stick cooking spray. Set aside.

In a mixer, cream together butter, sugar and eggs. Add sifted cake flour, baking powder and baking soda. Add sour cream and vanilla extract. Blend in chocolate chips.

Pour batter into a bundt pan sprayed with non-stick cooking spray and bake for 40 minutes in a preheated 350 degree oven. Test for doneness with a toothpick and continue baking up to 1 hour, if necessary. Cool for 1 hour and unmold. Sprinkle with confectioners sugar.

Freezes well.

AUNT FANNY'S NUT CAKE

This cake is a family favorite any time of the year!

PREHEAT OVEN TO 350 DEGREES

10   eggs, separated, room temperature
1¾   cups sugar
 ¾   cup orange juice
 1   cup matzo meal
 1   cup nuts, ground

....

Mix yolks with 1 cup sugar. Add orange juice, matzo meal and nuts. Blend well. In a separate bowl, beat egg whites until soft peaks start to form. Slowly add ¾ cup sugar and beat until stiff, but not dry. Fold in egg yolk mixture.

Pour batter into a greased tube pan. Bake for 1 hour and 10 minutes in a preheated 350 degree oven.

Let cool one hour, then invert onto a plate.

BLUEBERRY COFFEE CAKE

This coffee cake tastes like a cheese torte.

PREHEAT OVEN TO 350 DEGREES

Cake:
- 1½ cups flour
- ½ cup sugar
- ½ cup butter
- 1½ teaspoons baking powder
- 1 egg
- 1 teaspoon vanilla extract
- 1 quart blueberries

Topping:
- 2 cups sour cream
- 1 egg
- ½ cup sugar
- 1 teaspoon vanilla extract

1. Combine all ingredients for cake except blueberries. Mix well.

2. Pat into a 9 inch or 10 inch springform pan sprayed with non-stick cooking spray.

3. Sprinkle berries over the dough.

4. Combine ingredients for topping and mix well.

5. Pour topping over blueberries

Bake in a preheated 350 degree oven for 1 hour or until edge of custard is lightly browned. Cool for 1 hour before removing from pan.

Freezes well.

BLUEBERRY LEMON BUNDT CAKE

PREHEAT OVEN TO 350 DEGREES

1   package lemon cake mix
¾   cup vegetable oil
1   cup sour cream
4   eggs
1   heaping cup blueberries

Glaze:
1   cup confectioners sugar
1   tablespoon lemon juice

Spray a bundt pan with non-stick cooking spray.

Mix together cake mix with oil, eggs and sour cream. Gently fold in the blueberries. Spoon the batter into the prepared pan.

Bake in a preheated 350 degree oven for about an hour or until a toothpick comes out clean. Cool for 15 minutes. Unmold.

Prepare the glaze by mixing confectioners sugar with lemon juice. Drizzle over the cake. Eat, enjoy or freeze.

CARROT CAKE

Cake:
- 1½ cups butter
- 2 cups sugar
- 4 eggs
- 2 cups flour
- 1 heaping teaspoon cinnamon
- 2 teaspoons baking soda
- 3 cups packed shredded carrots with liquid
- 1 teaspoon vanilla extract
- ½ cup walnuts or pecans (optional)

Frosting:
- 6 ounces cream cheese, softened
- 1 cup butter, softened
- 1 16 ounce box confectioners sugar
- 2 teaspoons vanilla extract
- chopped walnuts (optional)

Cream butter and sugar. Add eggs and blend well. Sift flour, cinnamon and baking soda and add to batter. Add shredded carrots, vanilla extract and nuts.

Spray 2 round cake pans or 2 square 8 inch cake pans with non-stick cooking spray. Pour in batter and make sure it is evenly distributed. Bake in a preheated 350 degree oven for 45 minutes. The cakes will rise and then sink in center, so be sure to have enough batter in center.

Cool for 1 hour and frost between layers and on top.

This cake freezes well even with frosting.

To make frosting, mix cream cheese and butter. Slowly add confectioners sugar and beat until well blended. Add vanilla extract and stir until spreading consistency.

Optional: Sprinkle the top of the cake with chopped walnuts.

CHOCOLATE ENGLISH TRIFLE

Easy to prepare, impressive to serve!

- 1 chocolate cake (I bake a Duncan Hines Chocolate Fudge Cake in a 9 x 13 pan)
- 2 packages of chocolate pudding, prepared or 2 cans Thank You brand chocolate pudding
- 1 can (small) Hershey's Syrup
- 4 large bananas
- ½ cup chopped walnuts (optional)
- 1 12 ounce Cool Whip
- 1 Hershey Bar (shaved) or 1 – 16 ounce bag of mini-chocolate chips

1. Cut cake in half. Take half and cut into chunk pieces to cover bottom of glass bowl.
2. Cover with one can of pudding.
3. Drizzle ½ can of syrup on top of pudding layer.
4. Cover pudding layer with ½ of the sliced bananas and nuts.
5. Top with ½ of Cool Whip. Repeat the sequence beginning with chunks of cake and continue through the layer of Cool Whip. Sprinkle with the shavings of the Hershey bar or mini-chocolate chips.

This recipe is also great using banana cake, bananas, vanilla pudding and strawberries. Do not use Hershey's Syrup for this version.

/TWINKIE BERRY TRIFLE SURPRISE

 1 box (15.5 ounces) twinkies
 4 packages vanilla pudding, ready made
 1 8 ounce container Cool Whip
20 raspberries
40 blueberries
20 strawberries, sliced
 1 large strawberry for the top

Line a glass trifle bowl on the bottom with 5 Twinkies. Cover with 2 small container of vanilla pudding. Then cover with a layer of half of the berries. Cover the berry layer with half of the Cool Whip. Repeat the Twinkie layer, vanilla pudding layer, berry layer and top with a final layer of Cool Whip. Put one large strawberry in the middle and serve. Dreamy and delish!

P.S. For a chocolate trifle, use Hostess cupcakes and chocolate pudding.

COOKIE SHEET APPLE OR PLUM CAKE

This cake is made in a cookie sheet with sides. When prune plums are in season, I use them instead of the apples and it tastes like a plum kuchen.

PREHEAT OVEN TO 350 DEGREES

- 1 **cup butter**
- 1 **cup sugar**
- 2 **cups flour**
- 1 **egg**
- 1 **shot of bourbon (optional)**
- 72 **slices of apple (or...48 tiny plums cut in half. If using larger plums, cut in half and then into slices)**
  confectioners sugar for sprinkling on finished cake
  whipped cream or Cool Whip for garnish

Mix butter, sugar, flour, egg and bourbon together and place in refrigerator for 1 hour. While that is chilling, split the plums and pit them or slice the apples.

P.S. if you are using small apples you'll need more apple slices.

Pat dough into a cookie sheet with sides that is sprayed with non-stick cooking spray. Place apples or plums on top and line them in rows until all the dough is covered.

Bake in a preheated 350 degree oven until dough turns golden, approximately 30 minutes. When cool, sprinkle with confectioners sugar. Cut into squares and serve with whipped cream or Cool Whip on the side.

When in season, sliced fresh peaches are a delicious substitute.

Freezes well.

P.S. To make this a little fancier, melt 6 ounces of apricot preserves over low heat and cool slightly. Brush over the fruit slices. As an optional garnish, chop up pistachio nuts and sprinkle lightly down the center of each row, then bake according to directions. DO NOT FREEZE with the above additions.

DONNA'S ICE CREAM SUNDAE CAKE

A refreshing dessert that kids and adults love.

- **40 Oreo cookies**
- **6 tablespoons butter, melted**
- **½ gallon ice cream, any flavor, softened**
- **1 pound jar Smucker's Fudge Sauce**
- **1 cup nuts (optional)**

1. Crush cookies and stir together with melted butter.
2. Pat ¾ of crumbs into the 9 x 13 pan sprayed with non-stick cooking spray (reserve ¼ of crumbs for topping).
3. Pour softened ice cream on top of crumbs.
4. Freeze for 3 hours.
5. Pour fudge sauce over ice cream.
6. Sprinkle nuts over the entire cake.
7. Sprinkle extra crumbs over fudge and place back in freezer for another 45 minutes.
8. Remove from freezer a few minutes before serving.
9. Cut into squares as you serve.

CUPCAKE PARTY

My grandchildren love this fun idea. I have done it for their birthday parties.

- 1 box Duncan Hines Cake Mix, chocolate or white
- 1 package ice cream cones with flat bottoms
  variety of frostings and toppings

. . . .

PREHEAT OVEN TO TEMPERATURE ON BOX.

Prepare the cake mix according to the directions on the package.

Stand the cones in a cupcake pan, and fill each cone about 2/3rd full with cake mix. The mix will rise and fill the cone.

Bake to the time designated for cupcakes. Test with a toothpick until it comes out clean. Let them cool completely.

Set up a table with frostings, sprinkles, and candy pieces. Let the kids frost the cupcakes and decorate!

HEATH BAR ICE CREAM CAKE

- 3 packages lady fingers
- 6 pints vanilla ice cream
- 9 small Heath Bars, crushed
- 6 teaspoons instant coffee
- ½ pint heavy whipping cream
- ¼ cup confectioners sugar
- 2 tablespoons cocoa
- 1 can fudge sauce (optional)

This is made in a 8 or 9 inch spring form pan sprayed with non-stick cooking spray.

In a large bowl, softened ice cream. Sprinkle with instant coffee and crushed Heath bars. Mix well. Line sides and bottom of prepared spring form pan with lady fingers. Pour ½ of ice cream mixture on lady fingers. Add another layer of lady fingers on top of ice cream. Pour on the remaining ice cream.

Prepare topping by whipping up heavy cream with confectioners sugar and cocoa. Frost top of cake and put in freezer to harden.

Take cake out of freezer a few minutes before serving. Remove sides of spring form pan and serve with the fudge sauce on the side!

This is a beautiful, delicious treat!

COOKIE AND CREAM CHEESECAKE

I "dreamed" up this recipe one night when I couldn't sleep!

PREHEAT OVEN TO 350 DEGREES

1 box plain chocolate wafers, ground
⅓ cup butter, melted
1¼ cups sugar
3 8 ounce packages of cream cheese, softened
2 teaspoons vanilla extract
3 eggs
6 Oreo cookies, ground
1 cup sour cream

To prepare crust, chop chocolate wafers into small crumbs. Add melted butter and ¼ cup of sugar. Mix well and press into the bottom of a 8 or 9 inch spring form pan sprayed with non-stick cooking spray.

In a mixer beat cream cheese until fluffy. Add 1 cup sugar and vanilla extract. Beat in eggs, one at a time. Add ¾ of the Oreo cookie crumbs and stir until well blended. Add sour cream and mix well.

Pour over prepared crust and sprinkle top with remaining ¼ of Oreo cookie crumbs. Bake in a preheated 350 degree oven for 60-70 minutes. Turn off oven and leave cake in for an additional hour with the oven door ajar.

Remove from oven and cool for at least four hours or overnight. Remove side and serve or freeze.

P.S. A variation to this recipe is to double my "Shiny Chocolate Glaze" and spread it over the top and sides of the cooled cake. Then take 6 – 8 whole Oreo cookies and gently push them, standing on their sides, along the border of the top so most of the cookie is showing. This makes a very elegant presentation.

SHINY CHOCOLATE GLAZE

This recipe is used for regular cakes, brownies and it's great on some of the cheese cake recipes you find throughout the book.

½ **cup chocolate chips**
2 **tablespoons butter**
2 **tablespoons corn syrup**

. . . .

In a small saucepan, melt the chocolate chips, butter and corn syrup over low heat. When melted, spread over the cooled cake.

P.S. If you are covering a cheese cake, double the recipe.

/WHOOPIE PIES ANY WAY YOU WANT THEM

To make this recipe, you need to purchase a whoopee pie pan. You can find them in most cooking supply stores. It's worth it - these sandwich cake/cookies are incredible.

    1 **box cake mix, any flavor**

Filling:

    2 **cups confectioners sugar**

    ½ **cup butter**

    2 **teaspoons vanilla extract**

Spray whoopie pie pan with non-stick cooking spray.

Combine ingredients based on the package directions. Bake in the whoopie pie pan and set aside.

Combine the filling ingredients and beat well. This is a basic cream filling. It can easily be adjusted for different flavors. If you want carrot cake pies add 18 oz of (shredded?) carrots.

P.S. use this filling recipe as a frosting for your everyday cupcake.

LOUIS DELL'OLIO'S CHOCOLATE CHIP CHEESECAKE

Louis Dell'Olio is the highly respected designer for Anne Klein and Company. His sophisticated modern classics are the favorites of women all over the country. You'll love the "design" of this cheesecake!

PREHEAT OVEN TO 350 DEGREES

Cake:
- 1½ cups flour
- 1 cup sugar
- ¼ cup cocoa
- 1 teaspoon baking soda
- ½ teaspoon salt
- 1 cup water
- ½ cup vegetable oil
- 1 teaspoon vinegar
- 1 teaspoon vanilla extract

Topping:
- 1 8 ounce package cream cheese, softened
- 1 3 ounce package cream cheese, softened
- 1 egg
- ½ cup sugar
- ⅛ teaspoon salt
- 6 ounces semi-sweet chocolate chips

To make cake, blend all ingredients together. Batter may appear thin. Pour into 8 inch square pan that has been sprayed generously with non-stick cooking spray.

To make topping, mix cream cheese, egg, sugar and salt. Beat until well blended. Stir in chocolate chips. Drop by teaspoonfuls over cake layer and spread evenly.

Bake in a preheat 350 degree oven for 50 minutes. Cool and cut into squares.

WORLD'S BEST CHEESECAKE

I use this basic recipe for all my special, creamy cheesecakes.

PREHEAT OVEN TO 350 DEGREES

- 1¾ cups graham cracker crumbs
- ⅓ cup butter, melted
- 1¼ cups sugar
- 3 8 ounce packages of cream cheese
- 2 teaspoons vanilla extract
- 3 eggs
- 1 cup sour cream

Spray an 8 or 9 inch springform with non-stick cooking spray. Set aside.

To form the crust, blend graham cracker crumbs with melted butter and ¼ cup sugar. Press firmly into the prepared spring form.

In a mixer beat cream cheese until fluffy. Add 1 cup sugar and the vanilla extract. Beat in eggs, one at a time. Blend in sour cream.

Pour over prepared crust and bake for 60 – 70 minutes in a preheated 350 degree oven until firm then turn off oven and leave door ajar for an additional hour. Remove cake from oven and cool. Chill at least 4 hours or overnight in the refrigerator. Remove from spring form and serve or freeze until needed.

P.S. This makes a fabulous, plain cheesecake. To make it fancier, top the cake with a can of your favorite fruit pie filling. Personally I use cherry or blueberry. The cake looks beautiful and tastes great!

PEANUT BUTTER CUP CHEESECAKE

This recipe is another one of my nighttime inspirations.

PREHEAT OVEN TO 350 DEGREES

- 1 box chocolate wafer cookies, ground into crumbs
- ⅓ cup butter, melted
- 1¼ cups sugar
- 3 8 ounce packages cream cheese, softened
- 2 teaspoons vanilla extract
- 3 eggs
- ¼ cup peanut butter
- 1 cup sour cream
- 8 mini chocolate peanut butter cups (for garnish)

Glaze:
- ½ cup chocolate chips
- 2 tablespoons butter
- 2 tablespoons corn syrup

. . . .

To form crust, blend chocolate wafer crumbs, melted butter and ¼ cup sugar. Press mixture into an 8 or 9 inch spring form pan sprayed with non-stick cooking spray.

In a mixer, beat cream cheese until fluffy. Add 1 cup sugar and vanilla extract. Beat in eggs one at a time. Add the peanut butter and sour cream. Blend well.

Pour batter into prepared pan and bake in a preheated 350 degree oven for 60 – 70 minutes until light brown & set. Turn off the oven, but leave cake in the oven with the door ajar an additional hour. Remove from oven and cool. Chill for at least 4 hours or overnight.

To prepare glaze, melt chocolate chips, butter and corn syrup in a small sauce pan on low heat. Remove sides of the spring form and spread mixture on top of cheesecake. Place the peanut butter cups around the top of the cake in a circle with a little space in between.

PEANUT BUTTER CUP CHEESECAKE, cont.

This cake freezes well and is a dream for peanut butter lovers!

P.S. If you want to glaze the whole cake, double the recipe; and for additional beauty, stick a few more peanut butter cups on the side.

CREAM CHEESE CHERRY CUPCAKES

YIELD: 24   PREHEAT OVEN TO 350 DEGREES

- ¼ cup butter, melted
- 1 cup graham cracker crumbs
- 1 8 ounce cream, softened
- ¼ cup sugar
- 1 egg
- 1 can cherry pie filling

Melt butter and blend with graham cracker crumbs. Line mini muffin tins with paper cups, or spray with non-stick cooking spray.

Using a teaspoon, press a small amount of the crumb mixture into each cup.

In a mixer, blend cream cheese, sugar and egg until smooth. Spread this mixture over the crust until the cups are ¾'s full. Top with cherry pie filling and bake in a preheated oven for 10 minutes.

Remove from oven and cool in the refrigerator for at least 1 hour before serving.

This recipe freezes well!

PLUM DUMP CAKE

When a friend of mine gave me a piece of this cake to taste I couldn't believe that it was made with baby food. This cake is called a dump cake because you "dump" all the ingredients together and bake!

PREHEAT OVEN TO 350 DEGREES

Cake:
- 3 eggs
- 2 cups sugar
- 2 cups flour
- 1 cup oil
- 1 teaspoon cinnamon
- dash of ground cloves
- 3 teaspoons baking powder
- 1 cup chopped nuts (pecans or walnuts)
- 2 small jars of strained plum baby food

Glaze:
- 1 cup confectioners sugar
- juice of one lemon

. . . .

Mix all the cake ingredients together and pour into a sprayed bundt pan. Bake for 1 hour in a preheated 350 degree oven. Cool for 1 hour. Remove cake from pan.

To prepare glaze, mix confectioners sugar with juice. The glaze should be thick enough to drizzle. Use lemon juice to adjust thickness. Put in a measuring cup with spout and drizzle over cake.

SARAH'S POUND CAKE

This is a market favorite! It is wonderful marbleized with chocolate! You get two cakes from this recipe.

PREHEAT OVEN TO 325 DEGREES

1	pound butter
1	pound confectioners sugar
6	eggs
3	cups sifted cake flour
1½-2	tablespoons vanilla extract
2	squares unsweetened chocolate, melted (optional) or 2 prepared packages of melted chocolate

Cream butter and slowly add confectioners sugar. Drop in eggs, one at a time, until light and fluffy. Add sifted cake flour and vanilla extract. Continue to mix until well blended. Divide batter into 2 loaf pans. To marbleize cake, melt squares of chocolate and pour equally on top of batter. With a knife, cut through batter with a swirling motion.

Bake in a preheated 325 degree oven for 1 hour and 20 minutes. Let stand 5 minutes and then invert.

Freezes well.

SOUR CREAM CAKE

Cake:
- ½ pound butter
- 1 cup sugar
- 3 eggs
- 2½ cups all purpose flour, sifted
- 3 teaspoons baking powder
- 1 teaspoon baking soda
- 1 cup sour cream
- 1 teaspoon vanilla extract

Topping and filling:
- ½ cup sugar
- 1 teaspoon cinnamon
- 1 cup chopped nuts

Cream butter and gradually add sugar. Add eggs, one at a time. Sift together flour, baking powder and baking soda. Add to butter mixture and blend well. Add sour cream and vanilla extract and mix well.

In a separate bowl, mix together the sugar, cinnamon and nuts and set aside for filling and topping.

Spoon ½ of the cake batter into a sprayed 9 x 13 pan or tube pan. Cover with ½ of topping/filling mixture. Spoon other ½ of batter on top and then add rest of cinnamon-sugar topping.

Bake in a preheated 350 degree oven for 45 minutes. Test with a toothpick for doneness. Cool completely before cutting.

Freezes well.

APPLE CHEESE TORTE

This torte is always a huge hit. It's beautiful and delicious.

PREHEAT OVEN TO 350 DEGREES

Crust:
- ½ cup butter, room temperature
- ⅓ cup sugar
- ¼ teaspoon vanilla extract
- 1 cup all purpose flour

Filling:
- 1 8 ounce package cream cheese, room temperature
- ¼ cup sugar
- ½ teaspoon vanilla extract
- 1 egg

Topping:
- 4 cups apples, peeled and sliced (approximately 6 large apples)
- ⅓ cup sugar
- ½ teaspoon cinnamon
- confectioners sugar (optional)

· ·

To make crust, cream butter and sugar. Add vanilla extract. Add flour and mix well. Pat dough into bottom of a 9 inch spring for sprayed with non-stick cooking spray. Raise dough to about 2 inches on sides.

For topping: Toss sliced apples with sugar and cinnamon. Set aside.

In a large bowl combine filling ingredients until smooth. Pour filling into prepared crust.

Re-toss apples with cinnamon & sugar. Spread over the cream cheese filling. Bake for 35-45 minutes in a preheated 350 degree oven or until sides are lightly browned. Cool for 1 hour. Un-mold and dust with confectioners sugar.

P.S. Every oven is different. Watch carefully.

PLAIN OLD BANANA CAKE

PREHEAT OVEN TO 350 DEGREES

½	cup butter
1¼	cups sugar
2	eggs, lightly beaten
1	teaspoon baking soda
4	tablespoons sour cream
1	cup ripe bananas, mashed
1½	cups all purpose flour
1	teaspoon vanilla extract

In a mixer, cream butter and sugar. Add lightly beaten eggs and mix well. Stir in baking soda and sour cream. Beat well until blended. Add bananas, flour and vanilla extract. Mix well.

Pour batter into a 9 x 13 pan sprayed with non-stick cooking spray. Bake in a preheated 350 degree oven for one hour. Test with a toothpick.

When cool, cut into squares.

NUTTY CHOCOLATE CAKE

This cake freezes well and is very rich.

PREHEAT OVEN TO 350 DEGREES

1½	cups butter
6	eggs
1½	cups sugar
2	cups flour
1	package of powdered chocolate frosting mix
2	cups chopped walnuts

Cream butter in large bowl at high speed. Add eggs one at a time, beating well after each addition. Gradually add sugar and continue beating until light and fluffy. By hand, stir in flour, frosting mix and walnuts until well blended.

Pour batter into a sprayed or greased bundt pan. Bake in a preheated 350 degree oven for 60-65 minutes. Cool 2 hours before removing from pan.

SUNSHINE CAKE

You can bake this cake in a tube pan or in a 9 x 13. Either way, you'll love the delicious, delicate taste.

PREHEAT OVEN TO 325 DEGREES

Cake:

- 7 eggs, separated
- 1 teaspoon cream of tartar
- 1⅓ cups sugar
- 4 tablespoons hot water or orange juice
- 1 cup cake flour
- 1 teaspoon vanilla extract
- small can of shredded coconut (about 1½ cups)

Frosting:

Beat together:

- ½ cup butter
- 2 cups confectioners sugar
- 2 tablespoons milk
- 1 teaspoon vanilla extract

. . . .

Separate eggs into two bowls. Beat egg whites with cream of tartar and ⅔ cup sugar until fluffy. Set aside.

Beat egg yolks with ⅔ cup sugar and add hot water or orange juice. Add cake flour, vanilla extract and a handful of coconut. Carefully fold in egg whites.

Pour batter into a sprayed tube or 9 x 13 pan. Bake for 1 hour in a preheated 325 degree oven.

Cool for 1 hour and frost. Sprinkle rest of coconut over top of cake.

Freezes well even with the frosting.

APPLE CINNAMON BUNDT CAKE

This cake is delicious right out of the oven or four days later!

PREHEAT OVEN TO 350 DEGREES

Filling:
Mix together:

¼ cup sugar
3 large apples, sliced and peeled
½ tablespoon cinnamon, set aside

Cake Base:
Mix together:

2½ cups sugar
3 teaspoons baking powder
½ cup orange juice
2½ teaspoons vanilla extract
1 cup oil
4 eggs (lightly beaten)
3 cups unsifted flour
  nuts (optional)

Glaze: (optional)
Mix together:

1 cup confectioners sugar
1 teaspoon vanilla extract
3 tablespoons orange juice
1 teaspoon finely grated orange rind (optional)

In a greased bundt pan, pour ½ of cake base. Spread the apple mixture evenly over this layer. Then spread the other ½ of cake base mixture on top. Bake 1½ - 1¾ hours in a preheated 350 degree oven. Test for doneness with toothpick. Cool for 1 hour and then drizzle the glaze over the cake.

Freezes well.

LEMON POUND CAKE

Cake:
- 1 cup butter
- 2 cups sugar
- 3 eggs
- 3¼ cups cake flour
- ½ teaspoon baking soda
- 1 cup buttermilk
- 2 tablespoons grated lemon
- 2 tablespoons lemon juice or lemon extract

Glaze:
- ⅓ cup butter
- 2 cups confectioners sugar
- 2-4 tablespoons hot water
- ½ teaspoon lemon peel

Cream butter and sugar until light and fluffy. Beat in eggs, one at a time. Add cake flour, baking soda and buttermilk to the mixture and stir until well blended. Stir in grated lemon and lemon juice.

Pour into a sprayed bundt pan and bake for 1 hour in a preheated 325 degree oven. When a toothpick comes out clean, the cake is done. Cool for at least one hour and then invert. Before glazing, make sure the cake is totally cooled.

To prepare glaze, mix butter and confectioners sugar. Add hot water and lemon peel. Mix well. Drizzle glaze over cake. Allow glaze to harden before serving or freezing.

BEST RUM CAKE EVER!!

This recipe comes from my friend Verna in Hawaii. She serves it for all her parties and it's really a "smash"! **This one's just for laughs!**

1 or 2	quarts Rum
1	cup butter
1	teaspoon sugar
2	large eggs
1	cup dried fruit baking powder
1	teaspoon soda
	lemon juice
	brown sugar
	nuts

. . . .

Before you start, sample the Rum to check for quality. Good isn't it? Now go ahead.

Select a large mixing bowl, measuring cup, etc. Check the Rum again. It must be just right. To be sure Rum is of the highest quality, pour 1 level cup of rum into a glass and drink it as fast as you can. Repeat – with an electric mixer beat 1 cup butter in a large fluffy bowl, add 1 seaspoon of thugar and beat again.

Meanwhile, make sure that the Rum is of the finest quality. Try another cup. Open second quart if necessary. Add 2 arge eggs, 2 cups fried druit and beat till high. If druit gets stuck in beater, just pry it loose with a drewscriver.

Sample the Rum again, checking for tonscisticity. Next sift 3 cups of pepper or salt (it really doesn't matter). Sample the Rum again. Sift ½ pint of lemon juice. Fold in chopped butter and strained nuts. Add 1 babblespoon of brown thugar, or whatever color you find. Wix mel.

Grease oven and turn cake pan to 350 gredees. Not pur the whole mess into the coven, and ake. Check the Rum again, and go to bed.

JUST FOR STARTERS

JUST FOR STARTERS

AVOCADO MOLD

1	envelope unflavored Knox Gelatin
¼	cup cold water
2	packages frozen avocado dip, defrosted
1	mashed fresh avocado
1	6 ounce dry Italian seasoning dressing mix
1	pint sour cream
2	drops green food coloring
½	cucumber, peeled, seeded and chopped
½	can chopped black olives
½	pound cooked and cleaned baby shrimp
2	tablespoons caviar

Spray a 9½ inch tart pan with non-stick cooking spray.

In a small sauce pan, sprinkle gelatin over cold water. Let sit for 5 minutes to soften. Cook over medium heat until mixture just comes to a boil and gelatin dissolves.

In a large bowl, mix the avocado dips and fresh avocado with Italian seasoning, sour cream and green food coloring. Add prepared gelatin and mix together. Pour mixture into sprayed pan and refrigerate until firm. DO NOT FREEZE.

Unmold and garnish with chopped cucumbers in a circular motion bordering the outermost edges of the pan. Follow with a border of black olives. Then, move in towards the center with circles of shrimp. Put caviar in the center of mold. Serve with crackers.

It looks beautiful and tastes great.

P.S. The green food coloring is used to maintain the "avocado" color instead of the brownish green color caused when avocados are exposed to air.

ILENE'S SPINACH DIP

Fast and easy spinach dip to make in a jiffy.

- 10 ounce package frozen chopped spinach, defrosted (squeeze out excess water)
- 2 cups mayonnaise (I use Hellmann's)
- 5 green onions, chopped
- ⅓ cup fresh chopped parsley

Put all ingredients into a blender and mix well. Chill and enjoy.

This recipe looks great if you take a round bread and scoop out the middle and put spinach dip into center. Serve this with all your favorite vegetables for dipping.

GAZPACHO MOLD

My friend Barbara Adler gave me this recipe. I serve it with my Mexican lunch, but it's a great appetizer anytime!

- 2 envelopes unflavored gelatin
- ¼ cup cold water
- ¼ cup boiling water
- 2 cups mayonnaise (Hellmann's)
- 2 tomatoes, chopped and drained
- 1 green pepper, seeded and chopped
- 1 small onion, chopped
- 1 cup celery, chopped
   salt and pepper

Dissolve gelatin with ¼ cup cold water. Add ¼ cup boiling water and stir to dissolve. Mix gelatin with mayonnaise. Add tomatoes, green pepper, cucumber, onion and celery. Blend well. Add salt and pepper to taste. Grease (or spray) small, 4½ cup mold and pour in mixture. Chill at least 4 hours or overnight.

Run a knife carefully along sides of mold. Put a plate over the top and gently shake to unmold. This recipe slices well and can be served as a side dish.

SHRIMP MOUSSE

This is a favorite at market time. My friend Barbara gave me this recipe. It can easily be doubled.

1   envelope unflavored gelatin
⅓   cup cold water
1   cup tomato soup, not diluted
1   8 ounce cream cheese, softened
1   cup mayonnaise
2   4½ ounce cans tiny shrimp, mashed
½   cup celery, chopped
½   cup onion, finely chopped

Dissolve gelatin in ⅓ cup cold water. Set aside.

In a medium sized pot, bring soup to a boil. Add gelatin and stir well. Remove from heat.

Pour soup and gelatin mixture into a mixer and add softened cream cheese. Process until smooth. Stir in mayonnaise and add shrimp. Blend well. Add celery and onion and stir well.

Put mousse into a small 4½ cup mold sprayed with non-stick cooking spray.

Refrigerate for at least 4 hours or overnight. Unmold and serve with crackers.

CAVIAR MOLD

SERVES: 10 - 12

1	package unflavored gelatin
2	tablespoons lemon juice
2	tablespoons water
½	cup Hellmann's mayonnaise
½	cup Miracle Whip
2	tablespoons sour cream salt and pepper to taste
2	teaspoons Worcestershire sauce
1	4 ounce jar lumpfish caviar
½	small onion, grated
2	teaspoons anchovy paste
6	hard boiled eggs, chopped fine

Dissolve gelatin in small dish with lemon juice and water. Place dish in bowl of hot water until gelatin dissolves.

In another bowl, blend mayonnaise, Miracle Whip, sour cream, salt, pepper, Worcestershire sauce, caviar, onion and anchovy paste. Mix well by hand. Add chopped eggs and mix lightly but thoroughly. Stir in gelatin.

Use a 1½ pint ring mold that has been sprayed with non-stick cooking spray. Pour mixture into mold. Chill for 4 hours or more.

The mold can be made the day before.

Unmold and garnish with crackers or toast points.

This recipe can be doubled.

COLD CRABMEAT DIP

     2   packages frozen crabmeat, defrosted
     1   8 ounce cream cheese
     1   3 ounce cream cheese
     2   tablespoons mayonnaise (I use Hellman's)
     1   teaspoon Worcestershire sauce dash garlic powder
     1   teaspoon lemon juice
     1   whole chopped green onion
     1   bottle Hoffman's Shrimp Cocktail Sauce
     2   tablespoons chopped fresh parsley for garnishing
   1-2   drops lemon juice (optional)
         crackers for dipping

Defrost crabmeat and squeeze out any excess liquid. Set aside. In a mixer or Cuisinart with steel blade, blend cream cheese, mayonnaise, Worcestershire sauce, garlic powder, lemon juice and green onion. Process just until blended and creamy.

Put mixture into a round dish. Cover with cocktail sauce. Spread crabmeat on top and sprinkle enough parsley just to garnish. Sprinkle in a drop or two of lemon juice, if desired. Refrigerate at least 1 hour before serving. Serve with assorted crackers surrounding the dish. This is delicious and looks beautiful!

CRAB MEAT EGG DELIGHT

YIELD: 12 EGG HALVES

- 6 hard-boiled eggs
- 6 ounce crab meat, drained
- ½ stalk celery, roughly chopped
- 1 teaspoon mayo
- 1 teaspoon sour cream
- ⅛ teaspoon Lawry's Seasoned Salt
  salt and pepper to taste

Cut eggs in half, lengthwise. In a Cuisinart, mix egg yolks, crab, celery, mayo and sour cream. Add the seasoning. Fill egg white halves with mixture.

You can find the egg platters all over now. Deviled eggs are popular again!

GAZPACHO

My friend Marlene made this soup for me at market time when I served my Mexican lunch. It was a great hit.

- 3 19 ounce cans peeled whole tomatoes
- 6 cucumbers, peeled, seeded and chopped
- 6 green onions, chopped
- 1 green pepper, chopped
- 2 cloves garlic, chopped fine
- 2 stalks celery, chopped
- ½ cup olive oil
- ½ teaspoon dried dill weed
- 1 quart tomato juice
- ½ cup lemon juice, fresh squeezed (only)

Tabasco to taste dash to paprika

Optional:
- 2 teaspoons Lawry's Seasoned Salt
- 1 tablespoon sugar

Garnish:
- chopped parsley
- croutons
- chopped hard boiled egg

....

Using a Cuisinart, fitted with a steel blade, individually chop tomatoes, cucumbers, green onions, green pepper, garlic and celery. Place each in separate bowl.

Combine olive oil and dill weed and process for 30 seconds. Add all chopped vegetables and process with a few quick on/off pulse, just to blend.

Add tomato juice, lemon juice, Tabasco and paprika. If desired add Lawry's seasoned salt and sugar. Process until well blended and the consistency you enjoy. Pour into a large pitcher and chill for at least 1 hour before serving.

Serve in small bowls and mugs. Have chosen Garnishes available in individual bowls for your guests to top off their soup.

This is a hit as part of a Mexican dinner, on a hot summer day or anytime!

JOAN & GWEN'S SALMON MOUSSE

Joan Stemple and Gwen Levy have each made me this salmon mousse for every market. It's divine!

- 1   envelope unflavored gelatin
- ½   cup boiling water
- 2   tablespoons lemon juice
- 1   small onion, sliced
- ½   teaspoon salt
- ½   cup mayonnaise (I use Hellmann's)
- 1   16 ounce can red salmon, drained and boned
- 1   teaspoon dill weed
- ¼   teaspoon paprika
- ½   cup heavy cream
       cucumber for garnish

Mix gelatin with boiling water. Combine with lemon juice and onion in a blender or a Cuisinart fitted with steel blade. Process for 30 seconds. Add salt, mayonnaise, salmon, dill and paprika. Blend again, for 15 seconds. Add heavy cream and blend for an additional 15 seconds.

Pour into a sprayed 3 cup mold (fish mold is great). Cover with plastic wrap and refrigerate for at least 4 hours or overnight. Recipe may be made 2 days in advance. Unmold and decorate with sliced cucumbers.

P.S. Use the EASY CUCUMBER SAUCE on the side if desired!

NANCY AND DAVID'S RASPBERRY BAKED BRIE

Nancy and David design fabulous, innovative jewelry. Their contemporary silver pieces are worn with great pride. This brie recipe makes a terrific hors-d'oeuvre. This is my daughter Lizie's favorite recipe. She doesn't love to cook, but she loves to make this appetizer.

PREHEAT OVEN TO 350 DEGREES

- 1 package filo dough
- 1 mini brie
- 1 8 ounce jar raspberry preserves
- 1 3 ounce package almonds, sliced
- 4 tablespoons butter, melted

On a greased cookie sheet, spread several pieces of filo dough. Dough should be wide enough to completely cover brie.

Place brie in center of dough. Generously spread preserves on top of brie. Sprinkle sliced almonds over preserves.

Carefully lift filo dough to cover entire brie. If desired, crumble some additional filo dough on top to make crust flakier. Brush melted butter over entire crust.

Bake in a preheated 350 degree oven for 25 minutes. Remove from oven and let stand 10 minutes before serving.

SEAFOOD MOLD

SERVES: 10-12

 2 packages of Knox gelatin
 2 cans of crabmeat, drained, reserving 3 tablespoons of liquid
 1 can cream of mushroom soup, undiluted
 1 8 ounce Philadelphia cream cheese, softened
 1 can of shrimp, drained
 ¾ cup celery, chopped
 1 whole sweet onion, grated fine
 ¾ cup Hellmann's mayonnaise
    celery chunks, for garnish
    crackers

Take 3 tablespoons of the liquid from canned crabmeat and stir into the gelatin. Add mushroom soup and bring to a boil.

Add softened cream cheese and stir until thoroughly dissolved.

Slowly blend in crabmeat, shrimp, celery, onion and mayonnaise and mix thoroughly by hand.

Pour into a small fish mold sprayed with non-stick cooking spray and refrigerate.

Unmold by running a knife carefully around mold. Place plate over mold, invert and shake gently to remove.

Garnish with celery chunks and crackers.

MY FAMOUS 7 LAYER AVOCADO PIE

I use a large round Lucite platter that has a 1 inch lip all the way around. I've seen this done in throw-away foil pans. Adjust the increments of each ingredient depending on the size of the bowl. Thanks to Marsha Greenberg for this yummy recipe.

SERVES 40 PEOPLE

- 5 cans of Frito-Lay Bean Dip
- 4 cups sour cream
- 1 double package of taco seasoning (or 2 regular size)
- 7 cans frozen avocado dip, defrosted or avocado dip found in refrigerated section of the supermarket
- 3 cans sliced black olives
- 5 large tomatoes cut into small pieces and drained
- ½ cup chopped scallions (optional)
- 1 large package shredded cheddar cheese
- 2 bags nacho or taco chips for dipping

. . . .

Spread bean dip so it covers bottom of serving tray and just up the sides. Mix sour cream with taco seasoning and spread on top of bean dip to cover. Next, spread avocado dip over sour cream. Cover with olives, tomatoes and scallions. Finally, a layer of cheddar cheese.

Refrigerate overnight and enjoy with Nacho or Taco chips served on the side.

For a smaller group, cut the recipe in half

/VEGGIE CHOPPED LIVER

You won't believe it's not the real thing.

YIELD: 4 LARGE SANDWICHES

- 8 hard boiled eggs
- 1 medium onion, chopped
- 3 tablespoons vegetable oil
- 1½ cups chopped fine or diced walnuts
- 1 tablespoon mayonnaise
-    salt and pepper to taste

Boil eggs and cool them with cold running water. Peel the shell off of the eggs. Sauté the chopped onion in the vegetable oil. Place eggs, sautéed onions and walnuts in your food processor. Add mayo to bind the mixture. Season with salt and pepper to taste.

Refrigerate 1 hour and serve. This recipe is supposed to be refrigerated before serving, but many times people in my kitchen dig right in and it never makes it to the fridge.

VERNA'S CHEESE BALL

- 2 8 ounce packages cream cheese, softened
- 1 10 ounce package – extra sharp Cheddar cheese, grated (Cracker Barrel)
- 1 tablespoon green pepper, chopped fine
- 1 tablespoon onion, minced
- 1-2 dashes cayenne pepper (to taste)
- 1 teaspoon real lemon juice
- 1 teaspoon Worcestershire sauce
- 8 ounces walnuts, crushed

Mix together all ingredients except nuts and form 1 or 2 balls. Roll in crushed walnuts and chill. Can be frozen for later use.

SHRIMP PATÉ

1   3 ounce cream cheese (cut into cubes)
⅓   cup mayonnaise (I use Hellmann's)
3   tablespoons chopped onion
1   tablespoon white horseradish
1   teaspoon Dijon mustard
1   teaspoon dry dill
½   teaspoon sugar
½   teaspoon salt
1   tablespoon lemon juice
¼   teaspoon Tabasco sauce
¾   pound cooked and cleaned small shrimp cut into pieces (if canned, drain)
    assorted crackers

In a food processor, fitted with a steel blade, or a blender, process cream cheese and mayonnaise, just until smooth. Add onion, horseradish, mustard, dill, sugar, salt, lemon juice and Tabasco sauce and process until blended and smooth. Add shrimp and process until blended.   Remove mixture and shape into a ball. Wrap with wax paper and put in refrigerator for at least 4 hours or overnight. This can be prepared in advance and keeps for 3 days. Serve with assorted crackers.

SIMPLY SALADS

SIMPLY SALADS

COOKIE'S SALAD TOSS-UP TIPS!

1. Eggs should be fresh, clean and unbroken. Bad eggs can be harmful because the contain certain bacteria. Eggs are best used within one week of purchase, but can last in the refrigerator up to five weeks.
2. Always refrigerate any recipes with eggs. Bacteria grows quickly.
3. Hard boiled eggs should be used within one week.
4. Never try to freeze a recipe that includes mayonnaise. The mayonnaise will separate! Once a jar of mayonnaise is opened, keep the remainder refrigerated.
5. Never marinate vegetables or meats in a meat container. Only use glass or plastic.
6. Anything which needs to be marinated for more than 1 hour should be refrigerated.
7. I always put a little non-stick cooking spray into the pot of boiling water, before I add the pasta. It cooks beautifully!

CHINESE CHICKEN SALAD

SERVES 8 PEOPLE

- 2 pounds frozen chicken nuggets, breaded (found in freezer department or use leftover fried chicken cut into small pieces)
- 2 heads lettuce
- 1 can sliced water chestnuts, drained
- ¼ can bean sprouts
- ¼ pound pea pods cut in half
- 1 can or bag of chow mein noodles
- ¼ cup ketchup
- ¼ cup teriyaki sauce
- ½ cup honey
  fortune cookies (optional)
  melting chocolate (optional)

Bake chicken as directed. Let cool. If chunks are large, cut into small pieces. In a large bowl, shred lettuce and add water chestnuts, sprouts, pea pods and noodles. Add chicken chunks and toss. Mix together ketchup, teriyaki sauce and honey in a small bowl. Pour just enough sauce over chicken salad to lightly cover, but not drench the salad. Toss lightly.

This recipe is a favorite. It's wonderful to serve with the Oriental Pasta and Orange Ambrosia Jello.

For a special treat – dip fortune cookies in melted white or dark chocolate candy-making chocolate. Let dry on wax paper. Your company won't believe you did it.

CHICKEN SESAME SALAD

- 1 pound boneless cooked chicken, diced
- ¼ pound sugar snap peas
- ⅓ cup red pepper, chopped
- 1 8 ounce can water chestnuts
- ½ cup toasted almonds
- ¼ cup onion

Dressing:
- ½ cup vegetable oil
- 2 tablespoons soy sauce
- 3 tablespoons rice wine vinegar
- 3 tablespoons Hoisin sauce
- 1 teaspoon sesame oil
- 1 tablespoon teriyaki sauce

Chop all the vegetables and mix with the cooked chicken. Whisk together all the ingredients for the dressing. Coat the chicken and vegetables in the dressing. Serve the salad chilled.

P.S. You can always add more vegetables!

/ASIAN COLESLAW

Once you make this, it will become a favorite. The combination of the coleslaw with the crunchy noodles and nuts is a real winner.

Great for a Bar-B-Que!
- 1 16 ounce package Dole Coleslaw
- 1 cup slivered almonds
- 1 cup sunflower seeds (no shells)
- 1 tablespoon butter
- 1 bunch green onions, chopped
- 2 packages Chicken Ramen Noodles, crushed

Dressing:
- ½ cup olive oil
- ½ cup white vinegar
- ½ cup sugar

Sauté the seeds and nuts with 1 tablespoon butter over a low heat.

In a large bowl, mix the coleslaw, onions, nuts, seeds and noodles.

Whisk the dressing ingredients together in a small bowl. Pour dressing over salad just before serving.

ORIENTAL PASTA SALAD

I usually make 6 lbs. of this pasta recipe at a time! People can't get enough of it! Especially my son, Jason.

- 1   pound pasta, any shape you want (even plain spaghetti works great)
- 1   8 ounce bottle teriyaki sauce
- 2   tablespoons soy sauce
- 2½ tablespoons sesame oil
- 1   can sliced water chestnuts
- ¼   pound fresh pea pods, broken in half
- ¼   cup fresh bean sprouts

Prepare the pasta according to the directions on the package. Rinse with cold water and allow to come to room temperature.

Mix together teriyaki sauce, soy sauce and sesame oil. Add water chestnuts, pea pods and bean sprouts and stir together. Add prepared pasta and toss gently.

Refrigerate this recipe until cold. Then serve as a delicious side dish, lunch entrée or part of a buffet. It will stay in the refrigerator up to four days.

CHINESE BEANS

This is terrific to serve with my Chinese Chicken Salad!

- 2 pounds fresh raw string beans, broken in half
- ¾ cup teriyaki sauce (I use low-salt)
- 2 tablespoons sesame seeds
- 1 tablespoon sesame oil

Mix the teriyaki sauce, sesame seeds and oil in a bowl. Pour over beans and marinate in the refrigerator overnight. The flavor is wonderful.

CHICKEN SALAD DIVINE

When we first started our business, I chose my mother's chicken salad recipe for my first luncheon. In fact, I have memories of my parent's sitting in my kitchen taking apart chickens for hours. I still use this delicious recipe today...but I've gotten smart. Now I use just chicken breasts!

10	skinless chicken breasts (with or without bone)
3	stalks of celery
¾-1	cup Hellmann's Mayonnaise
1-3	ounce bag sliced almonds
20	green or red seedless grapes, cut in half Lawry's Seasoned Salt

Boil chicken breasts in a large pot of water until white and tender (approximately 20 minutes). Drain chicken and let cool (if you'd like, reserve the broth for a future chicken soup). Cut into small chunks.

Chop celery into bite-sized chunks and add to chicken. Stir in mayonnaise to coat. Add nuts and grapes and stir gently. Season with Lawry's salt to taste. Mix gently.

Chill in refrigerator at least one hour before serving. Easy and delicious!

EGG SALAD SUPREME

I used to make 18 dozen eggs into an egg salad mold for every market. When I'm asked for the recipe, my buyers think I'm leaving out something because it seems too easy to be so delicious. The secret is to make sure you use a Cuisinart or blender for chopping eggs.

SERVES 6 – 8 PEOPLE

- 1 **dozen eggs**
- 5 **tablespoons Hellmann's mayonnaise**
- 1 **teaspoon Lawry's Seasoned Salt**
  dash of pepper
  sour cream for garnish
  Lumpfish caviar for garnish (red –or– black)

Boil eggs and peel. Place in a food processor fitted with steel blade. Using the on/off button chop eggs into small fine pieces. Do not overprocess. Add mayonnaise, Seasooned Salt and pepper. Stir just to combine.

Spray a 6-cup ring mold or small springform pan with non-stick cooking spray and spoon in egg salad. Pat down, then chill overnight. Unmold on a platter and put sour cream into the hole and cover top of the sour cream with lumpfish caviar.

Looks fabulous! Tastes great!

P.S. I always pat the caviar so it doesn't bleed onto the sour cream.

TUNA SALAD MOUSSE

I have stores that come in specifically for my tuna. It's so popular, I make 30 pounds at each market.

- 2 stalks of celery, chopped fine
- 2 large cans water packed tuna
- 5 rounded tablespoons Hellmann's mayonnaise
- ½ teaspoon Lawry's Seasoned Salt dash of pepper

In a Cuisinart, fitted with a steel blade, chop stalks of celery. Squeeze excess water out of celery and set aside. Drain tuna well, and add to squeezed celery. Process in a Cuisinart with quick on/off pulses until almost smooth. Add mayonnaise and seasoning and stir by hand. Refrigerate at least 1 hour before serving.

Very easy – very good!

SANDWICH LOAF

I make these sandwich loaves at least twice a year. They look great on a platter. When my buyers slice into them, they think it's a layer cake.

SERVES 12 – 14

Loaf:
16 inch unsliced long loaf of bread (white, whole wheat or mixed wheat are best.)
    Chicken Salad Divine
    Tuna Mousse
    Egg Salad Supreme
       (Refer to individual recipes)

Frosting:
½ cup Hellmann's mayonnaise
3 8 ounce packages of cream cheese

Garnish (optional):
2-3 chopped hard boiled eggs
1 can sliced green olives
1 can sliced black olives
1 large cucumber, thinly sliced

Remove the crust from a 16 inch long loaf of unsliced bread (you can order that size from any bakery). Turn loaf on side and cut into 4 even lengths. Spread each layer with a different salad. Use chicken salad, tuna salad and egg salad. Ham salad is also very good as one of the layers.

Prepare frosting by combining the mayonnaise with cream cheese. Mix well by hand or put into Cuisinart fitted with a steel blade to get a smooth consistency, Spread over the whole loaf. Decorate with sliced hard boiled eggs, sliced olives, and/or sliced cucumbers.

Refrigerate for at least one hour before serving.

LEFTOVER LAYERED SALAD

        Tuna salad
        Egg salad
        Salmon salad
1-2 cans frozen avocado spread, defrosted
½   teaspoon Good Season's Italian Dressing
8   ounces sour cream red or black caviar for garnish

Spray non-stick cooking spray in a spring form pan large enough to hold your left-over salads. Layer salads one on top of the other, smoothing after each addition.

In a separate bowl, mix together ½ teaspoon of the Good Season's powdered dressing for each can of avocado spread that you use. The quantity will depend on the size of your pan.

Spread avocado mixture over salads. Refrigerate for 2 hours. Add a layer of sour cream and refrigerate for another few hours or overnight.

Before serving, put a dollop of caviar in the center or cover the entire top with caviar.

Unmold and serve with toast points and crackers.

Easy and delicious!

P.S. If you can't find the frozen avocado spread just blend a fresh avocado with a few drops of green food coloring. This keeps the color from turning brown. Then spread as directed.

TAFFY APPLE SALAD

I always double this recipe for my market. It takes 2 days to put it together, but it's worth the time! See below for a quick version that is delicious too!

- 1 large can pineapple chunks in heavy syrup separate juice in one pot, chunks in another.
- 2 cups mini-marshmallows
- 1 tablespoon flour
- 1½ tablespoons white-plain vinegar
- 1 egg
- ½ cup sugar
- 1 8 ounce Cool Whip
- 1½ cups Planter's Cocktail Peanuts
- 4 peeled apples, red or green or a combination, cut in chunks

1. Place pineapple chunks and marshmallows together in a pot and cover. Place in refrigerator overnight.
2. Cook pineapple juice, flour, vinegar, egg and sugar over medium heat until thickens. Stir constantly. Refrigerate overnight (pick small pieces of white from egg out of cooked mixture).
3. On second day, mix steps 1 and 2 together.
4. Add Cool Whip, nuts and apples to mixture.
5. Refrigerate until serving. It really tastes like a taffy apple.

P.S. If you are in a hurry you can improvise with a container of Cool Whip. Add drained cans of fruit cocktail, chunks of apples, peanuts and shredded coconut. Yummy!

TACO SALAD

South of the border flavor in your own home.

SERVES 8

- 2 heads lettuce
- 2 large tomatoes, chopped and drained
- 1½ pounds ground beef
- 1 package taco seasoning
- ½ large bottle Catalina dressing
- 1 4 ounce package shredded cheddar cheese
- ¼ bag taco chips, crushed

Shred lettuce in a bowl. Add chopped tomatoes. In a large fry pan, brown ground beef and drain off fat. Stir in taco seasoning. Add beef to lettuce and tomatoes and toss with Catalina dressing. Top with cheddar cheese and crushed taco chips.

If you want to serve the salad warm, put it out immediately. If you want the salad to be cold, prepare the beef and chill it in the refrigerator. Then assemble with the rest of the cold vegetables, dressing, cheese and chips before serving.

MEXICAN RICE SALAD

1   8 ounce box white rice
1   can garbanzo beans, drained
1   red pepper, chopped
1   green pepper, chopped
2   tablespoons scallions, chopped
1   8 ounce jar Catalina dressing

Cook rice according to package directions. Let cool and then toss in a large bowl with garbanzo beans, red pepper, green pepper, scallions and Catalina dressing.

Refrigerate until thoroughly chilled. Will stay fresh in the refrigerator for 3 days.

CORN SALAD WITH OLIVES

2 bags frozen niblets corn
1 green pepper, chopped
1 red pepper, chopped
1 can sliced black olives
1 8 ounce bottle Italian dressing

Mix all ingredients together and chill overnight. The flavor is delicious and makes a great side dish.

THE BEST CAESAR SALAD

My friends in Florida tell me this is one of the favorites in the book.

    1   Romaine lettuce washed and chilled

Dressing:

    1   can flat anchovies

    2   cloves garlic

    ¼   cup olive oil

    1   egg

        salt and pepper

    1   cup freshly grated
        Parmesan cheese

   8+   croutons

Drain anchovies and put in bottom of a small bowl. Press cloves of garlic through press and mix with anchovies. Make into a paste by pressing with a fork into bottom and sides of bowl. Add olive oil a little at a time and continue mixing. Squeeze juice of a whole lemon with a fork into the mixture. Coddle the egg by boiling in water for 30 seconds. Add egg into mixture and stir.

Break chilled lettuce into small pieces. Just before serving pour dressing over the lettuce. Add salt, pepper to taste and lightly sprinkle with parmesan cheese. Add croutons and toss lightly!

Serve and enjoy!

ANTIPASTO PASTA SALAD

A very colorful presentation and delicious taste.

1	pound pasta, any shape

Cut into bite-size pieces:

1	cup mozzarella cheese
4	slices of salami
½	cup red pepper
½	cup green pepper
½	cup yellow pepper can of baby corn
1	medium zucchini
1	8 ounce bottle of Kraft Italian Dressing
	sprinkle with Parmesan cheese to taste

Mix all ingredients together. Chill thoroughly and serve.

EVERYDAY POTATO SALAD

SERVES 10

- 5 pounds red potatoes, peeled, boiled and cooled
- 6 hard boiled eggs, cooked and sliced
- 2 stalks celery, cut into small chunks
- 1 cup small frozen peas
- 2 cups mayonnaise (I use Hellmann's)
- 2 teaspoons Lawry's Seasoned Salt

Peel potatoes and boil them in a large pot of water approximately 15 minutes. When a fork is easily inserted, yet potatoes are still firm, they are done. Allow them to cool and then cut into bite-size chunks or slices. Add eggs, celery and peas. Mix together mayonnaise and seasoning salt and add potatoes. Mix well and refrigerate at least 1 hour before serving.

EASY AVOCADO PASTA

1 pound pasta, any size or shape
2 fresh avocados, peeled and cut into chunks
2 tomatoes, cut into chunks
1 bottle vinaigrette or Italian dressing (or use the Mustard Vinaigrette recipe in this book)

Cook pasta according to package directions. Drain and rinse with cold water. Put into large bowl and add avocados, tomatoes, and dressing. Toss gently and serve. Will stay fresh in refrigerator for 2 days.

✍ WATERMELON, HEIRLOOM TOMATO AND FETA SALAD

This is a quick and easy salad that tastes really refreshing. The flavors blend in unexpected ways. Love the salty feta with the yummy watermelon and basil. Sounds strange...but tastes delicious!

- 3 tablespoons extra-virgin olive oil
- 2 tablespoons chopped basil
- 1 tablespoon fresh lemon juice
- ½ teaspoon kosher salt
- 4 heirloom tomatoes, cut into chunks
- 2 cups (1-inch) cubed red seedless watermelon
- ¼ cup vertically sliced red onion (optional)
- ½ cup crumbled feta cheese
- 1/3 cup currants or other sweet raisins
- 1/2 cup sugared almonds or walnuts (optional)
- balsamic glaze (optional)

Whisk together first four ingredients in a large bowl. Add tomato, watermelon and onion; toss to mix well. Sprinkle with cheese, raisins and nuts. Toss again to coat ingredients.

**If there is yellow watermelon available, substitute 1 cup of that variety.*

P.S. If you have some balsamic glaze, allow your guests to drizzle a small amount over the salad. Gives the salad an extra kick.

TANGY COLD VEGETABLE SALAD

SERVES 10 – 12

- 2 cups broccoli
- 2 cups cauliflower
- 2 cups carrots
- 2 cups celery
- 2 cups zucchini
- 2 cups pea pods
- 1 cup red pepper
- 1 cup green pepper
- 1 large bottle Italian Salad Dressing
- 1½ pounds pasta, spirals
- 1 bottle chili sauce
- 2 tablespoons lemon juice
- 6 tablespoons Dippity-Dill mix or dry Hidden Valley Ranch packet

Chop up all vegetables into bite-size pieces. In a large bowl, marinate vegetables in Italian dressing overnight.

The next day, prepare pasta according to the package instructions. Drain and rinse with cold water. Drain marinade from vegetables, reserving ½ cup of dressing, and toss lightly with pasta.

Combine chili sauce, lemon juice and Dippity-Dill in a small bowl. Pour over pasta and vegetables and toss to coat. Add remainder of Italian marinade to taste.

Refrigerate until thoroughly chilled and serve!

CAESAR SALAD PASTA

This is such an easy salad to prepare, but one that everyone loves. I like to make the pasta ahead of time. The flavors mix so well together!

1   pound pasta, any shape
1   8 ounce bottle Caesar dressing – or see The Best Caesar Salad Dressing recipe
1   Romaine lettuce, rinsed well and chopped into chunks
1   box croutons
    grated parmesan cheese: to taste

Cook pasta according to directions. Drain and rinse with cold water. Add dressing, lettuce, croutons and cheese. Toss and serve. This is a wonderful addition to any meal or serve by itself.

QUICK SEAFOOD PASTA

1 pound pasta, shell shaped
1 pound small cooked and cleaned shrimp or crab meat, cut into chunks
   (or use artificial seafood sticks)
¼ pound little frozen peas, defrosted
3 celery stalks, cut into chunks
1 cup mayonnaise (Hellmann's)
3 tablespoons ketchup
   (Instead of mayonnaise and ketchup, an 8 ounce bottle of Russian
   dressing may be used)

Cook pasta according to package directions, drain and rinse with cold water. Put pasta in a large bowl. Add chunked seafood, peas and celery and stir. Combine mayonnaise and ketchup. Pour dressing over pasta and chill for 4 hours or overnight.

TORTELLINI PASTA ITALIANO

  1½   pounds tri-color tortellini pasta (or any tortellini)
    1   bottle Seven Seas Viva Herbs & Spices Dressing
    1   package frozen small Le Sur Peas
    1   red pepper, chopped into small pieces
  ¼   pound salami, cut into strips

Prepare tortellini according to package instructions. Drain and rinse well. Add remaining ingredients to the pasta and stir to coat.

Refrigerate for at least 4 hours before serving.

This is quick, easy and delicious!

SWEET COLD NOODLES

This is a great cold pasta. I made this one up when I was in the mood for something semi-healthy as well as something sweet.

    1   pound broad egg noodles
    1   pound cottage cheese
    1   cup sugar
    2   tablespoons cinnamon
    1   cup raisins

Cook pasta according to package directions. Drain and rinse with cold water. Pour into large bowl and mix in cottage cheese, sugar, cinnamon and raisins. Chill overnight and enjoy.

SNAPPY POTATO SALAD

This potato salad looks very festive and tastes superb!

SERVES: 10 PEOPLE

- 5   pound bag red potatoes
- 1   bottle Seven Seas Viva Herbs and Spices Dressing
- 1   3 ounce jar capers, drained
      fresh parsley, chopped (approximately ½ cup)
- 1   whole cabbage for garnish – red or purple

Boil potatoes in a large pot of water for approximately 45 minutes until a fork is easily inserted into potatoes and yet they are still firm. Do not remove potato skins. When cool, cut into bite-sized pieces and place in a large bowl. Add dressing, capers and just enough chopped parsley for color. Stir well to coat.

Line a bowl with the cabbage leaves for color and fill with potato salad.

MUSTARD VINAIGRETTE

1 clove garlic, minced
  -or-
1 clove shallot
¾ cup safflower oil
¼ cup vinegar
½ teaspoon salt
½ teaspoon sugar (or sugar substitute)
3 tablespoons water
2 tablespoons Dijon mustard

In a blender or food processor equipped with a steel blade, mince garlic or shallot. Add oil, vinegar, salt, sugar, water and Dijon mustard and process until well blended.

This dressing is delicious poured over salads or used as a marinade for chicken.

Refrigerate after preparing and shake well before serving.

LORENZO DRESSING

Many private clubs serve this dressing. Now it is available for your home use!

- 1 bunch watercress
- 4 ounces chili sauce
  Tabasco sauce – to taste
- 1 teaspoon Worcestershire sauce
- 2 cups salad oil
- ½ cup apple cider vinegar
- 1 teaspoon salt (or to taste)
- ⅛ teaspoon white pepper (or to taste)

Using a food processor fitted with a steel blade, or a blender, chop up watercress and then add rest of ingredients. Blend until smooth.

Chill well before using!

FANCY STEAK SALAD

My buyers think I'm serving the most extravagant lunch when I serve this salad!!

- 1 green pepper
- 3 cups broccoli
- 3 cups fresh pea pods
- 3 pounds flank steak, cut into strips
- 6 tablespoons peanut oil
- 1 8 ounce bottle teriyaki sauce
- 2½ tablespoons sesame oil
- 1 small can water chestnuts, sliced and drained

Wash, dry and cut green pepper, broccoli and pea pods into bite-sized pieces. Set aside.

Sauté the steak in peanut oil until meat is tender and browned. Drain excess fat. Add teriyaki sauce, sesame oil and stir to coat meat.

Pour meat into large bowl with vegetables and add water chestnuts. Toss to mix and refrigerate 4 hours or overnight.

Salad should be served very cold!

MOROCCAN COUSCOUS SALAD

Couscous has become a staple in the salad world. This could also be made with quinoa, the newest "darling" of the "protein" world. Be sure to cook the couscous ahead of time and put it in the refrigerator to get cold. Then add the other ingredients. If you are not a vegetarian, cut up grilled chicken is a great addition!

SERVES 12

- 1 10 ounce box couscous (Moroccan pasta)
- 1 16 ounce bottle Italian dressing
- 1 cup bite-size pieces green pepper
- 1 cup bite-size pieces red pepper
- 1 cup bite-size pieces chick peas
- 1 cup bite-size pieces mushrooms

Cook couscous according to package directions. Stir in Italian dressing. Add vegetables and mix well. Refrigerate overnight.

ALWAYS ROOM FOR JELLO

ALWAYS ROOM FOR JELLO

THINGS TO KNOW ABOUT JELLO!

It's probably been a long time since you've thought of serving jello as a side dish or dessert. You'll be surprised at the delightful reaction you'll receive when serving jello molds. They are delicious, refreshing and beautiful to serve.

Here are a few "tips" to help make your jello turn out just right!

1. Spray your molds with non-stick cooking spray. This will help them to come out easily.
2. Any recipe that calls for "sour cream" can use Cool Whip as a substitute in equal amounts. Any recipe made with Cool Whip can remain in the refrigerator up to 1 week.
3. Be sure the jello does not get hard before you are to add other ingredients. It should only be just starting to thicken.
4. To help quicken the "thickening" process, I often place the bowl in the freezer for a few minutes. Watch it because it starts to gel quickly. Also, you never want ice particles to form.
5. To create a "marbleized jello" choose a few favorite flavors. Chill until slightly thickened and whip with 1 cup of Cool Whip for a 6 ounce size jello. Pour the flavors into a greased bundt pan in layers. Then take a knife and swirl it through the layers in an "S" pattern. Chill for at least 4 hours, then unmold and serve.

CHOCOLATE BOTTOM RASPBERRY FLUFF

This creates a beautiful presentation and has a delicate, delicious taste!

Bottom:
- 1 package chocolate wafers, crushed
- ½ cup sugar
- ⅓ cup melted butter
- 1 large package raspberry Jello
- 2 cups boiling water
- 1 cup orange juice
- ½ cup sugar
- 1 large can Pet Evaporated Milk, chilled
- ½ box frozen raspberries (defrost and drain juice well)

Mix together chocolate wafers, sugar and melted butter and pat ¾'s of mixture into spring form pan sprayed with non-stick cooking spray.

Blend Jello with boiling water and add orange juice and sugar. Chill for ½ hour. In a mixer, beat evaporated milk into peaks. Add chilled Jello and raspberries. Beat until raspberry color comes through.

Pour into crust and sprinkle with remaining ½ of cookie crumbs. Chill thoroughly, at least 4 hours or overnight. Remove sides of spring form and serve.

HAWAIIAN DELIGHT

2 packages cherry Jello
2 packages lemon Jello
4 cups hot water
2 pints vanilla ice cream
2 cups sour cream
1 can sliced pineapple rings, drained
1 jar maraschino cherries

In two separate bowls, place cherry Jello and lemon Jello. Add 2 cups hot water to each and stir to dissolve. Chill until slightly thickened.

Whip each Jello separately. To each, add 1 pint of ice cream and 1 cup of sour cream. Beat well.

Place lemon Jello in sprayed bundt pan first. Put pineapple slices on top of whipped lemon Jello. Place a cherry in the center of each pineapple slice.

Pour whipped cherry Jello over pineapple slices and gently smooth to fill pan.

Refrigerate at least 4 hours or overnight.

Unmold and garnish with remaining fruit.

LEMON MOUSSE JELLO

I can't make a dinner without including this Jello, even my son-in-law expects it.

- 1 6 ounce package lemon Jello
- 2 cups boiling water
- 2 cups cold water
- 1 small carton lemon yogurt
- 1 12 ounce Cool Whip
  fresh strawberries, for garnish

Make lemon Jello as directed and chill until not quite firm. Add lemon yogurt and whip in the Cool Whip. Pour into a bundt pan sprayed with non-stick cooking spray or spoon into a bowl and refrigerate for 3 hours or overnight.

Unmold by running a knife gently around the edges and turn over on a platter. Shake gently to remove from pan. Garnish with fresh strawberries.

FINGER JELLO

This recipe comes from my friend Toddy. These are fun to take on a picnic!

YIELD: 100

- 4 envelopes Knox unflavored gelatin
- 3 boxes flavored Jello (3 ounce size), any flavor
- 3 cups boiling water

In a large bowl combine Knox unflavored gelatin and 3 flavored Jellos. Add boiling water and stir until dissolved. Pour into a large cookie sheet, with sides, that has been sprayed with non-stick cooking spray. Chill until firm.

Cut Jello into small squares. These can be picked by hand and eaten like candy. Children love them. Adults can't stop eating them.

ORANGE AMBROSIA JELLO MOLD

- 1 6 ounce orange Jello
- 2 cups boiling water
- 1 pint frozen orange sherbet
- 2 small cans mandarin oranges, drained
- 2 small cans pineapple chunks, drained
- ½ cup mini marshmallows
- ½ cup flaked coconut
- 1 cup sour cream

In a large bowl, dissolve Jello with 2 cups boiling water. Add frozen sherbet and mix until dissolved. Add mandarin oranges and pineapple chunks and refrigerate until thickened, but not set. Mix marshmallows, coconut and sour cream and combine with Jello. Chill again until firm. Pour into a sprayed or greased 6 cup Jello mold (or into a large glass bowl) and chill 9 hours or overnight.

You can do basically the same recipe using raspberry sherbet and raspberries instead of mandarin oranges.

I triple this recipe for a large crowd and put it into institutional size, 24 cup mold.

RASPBERRY MOUSSE JELLO

1	6 ounce raspberry Jello
2	cups boiling water
2	cups cold water
1	8 ounce carton raspberry yogurt
½	bag frozen raspberries, without juice (Wilderness brand if possible), defrosted
	-or-
1	cup fresh raspberries
1	12 ounce Cool Whip

Dissolve Jello and chill until almost firm. Add yogurt, raspberries and Cool Whip and whip together. Pour into a bundt pan sprayed with non-stick cooking spray, or spoon into individual glasses or bowls.

Chill for at least 4 hours or overnight.

Options:
    peach Jello and peaches
    cherry Jello and cherries
    strawberry/banana Jello and fruit

make sure to use the same flavor for the yogurt and Jello

To makes chocolate filigree garnish, as shown on cover:

3	ounces chocolate
	few drops vegetable oil
	parchment paper

Melt chocolate over double boiler. Smear back of cookie sheet with vegetable oil and smooth a sheet of parchment paper onto it.

cont.

RASPBERRY MOUSSE JELLO, cont.

Scrape chocolate into plastic bag. Cut tiny hole at corner. Pipe out filigree designs. Increase size of hole to achieve desired effect.

Set chocolate in cool place to harden. Do not refrigerate. Gently peel off parchment to free pieces.

ORANGE PINEAPPLE MOLD

- 1 6 ounce frozen orange juice undiluted, defrosted
- 2 3 ounce packages orange gelatin
- 1 pint sour cream
- 4 tablespoons marshmallow cream fluff
- 1 large can crushed pineapple with juice

In a medium saucepan, bring orange juice, orange gelatin, sour cream and marsh-mallow cream to a boil. Stir constantly until all ingredients are dissolved and smooth.

Remove from heat. Add can of crushed pineapple juice and stir until blended.

Pour into sprayed 6½ cup mold and chill in refrigerator at least 4 hours or overnight.

SOME LIKE IT HOT!

SOME LIKE IT HOT!

OSCAR DE LA RENTA'S LEMON CHICKEN

Oscar de la Renta is certainly one of the elite of the American fashion design community. His glamorous, elegant creations make every woman who wears them feel like a star. This is a quick and easy recipe for a wonderfully light and tasty dish!

SERVES 4

- 4 boneless, skinless breasts of chicken
- 1 cup chicken broth
- ¼ cup olive oil
- 2½ cups fresh lemon juice
- 1 tablespoon scallions
- 3 tablespoons cilantro
- 1 tablespoon white wine vinegar

Cut each chicken breast into four long pieces. Place chicken and broth in frying pan and cook on medium heat for ten minutes. Remove chicken and place in serving dish.

To broth, add olive oil, lemon juice and scallions and bring to a boil. Simmer for one minute and pour over chicken.

Sprinkle cilantro and white wine vinegar over dish to taste.

BING CHERRY DUCK

A dish that's guaranteed to be all it's "quacked" up to be.

PREHEAT OVEN TO 325 DEGREES

1   rack for roasting
1   duck quartered
    Lawry's Seasoned Salt
    paprika
1   can dark pitted cherries in sauce
1   tablespoon cornstarch

Spray roasting pan and rack well with non-stick cooking spray.

Place quartered duck on rack. Place rack in roasting pan and season with Lawry's and paprika. Roast duck for at least 4 hours in a preheated 325 degree oven until all the grease is on pan bottom and duck is dry and crispy.

In a heavy pot, heat can of cherries. Add corn starch and stir until sauce thickens. Pour sauce over quartered duck and serve with brown rice or wild rice.

A favorite green vegetable completes this beautiful plate.

BILL BLASS' MEAT LOAF

Bill Blass is one of 7ᵗʰ Avenue's most respected designers and one of the major forces in the fashion industry. However, when asked for his recipe he replied, "I may not go down in history for my clothes – but this meat loaf will be my claim to immortality!"

SERVES 6   PREHEAT OVEN TO 350 DEGREES

- 1 cup celery, chopped
- 1 cup onions, chopped
- 2 tablespoons butter
- 2 pounds chopped sirloin
- ½ pound veal, ground
- ½ pound pork, ground
- ½ cup parsley
- ⅓ cup sour cream
- 1½ cups bread crumbs (soft)
- 1 egg, beaten
- 1 tablespoon Worcestershire sauce
- pinch thyme
- pinch marjoram
- salt and pepper to taste
- 1 bottle Heinz chili sauce
- 3 strips bacon

Saute celery and onions in butter. Combine sirloin, veal and pork. Add remaining ingredients and form loaf. Top with chili sauce and bacon strips.

Bake in a preheated 350 degree oven for one hour.

Serve with crisp baked potato skins.

DIET CHICKEN DELIGHT

Everyone likes a diet dinner once in a while and this one is a goody.

SERVES 6   PREHEAT OVEN TO 350 DEGREES

- 4 chicken breasts split, boned and skinned
- 1 8 ounce bottle of low-calorie Italian dressing
  seasoning salt
- 2 Idaho potatoes, peeled and cut into pieces lengthwise
  sprinkle of Parmesan cheese (optional)
- 1 package of frozen Le Sur Peas, defrosted

In a 9 x 13 ovenproof glass dish, marinate the chicken in Diet Italian Dressing overnight. The next day, sprinkle the chicken with seasoning salt. Add potatoes and turn to coat well with dressing.

Bake in a preheated 350 degree oven for 30 minutes. Turn chicken and continue cooking an additional 30 minutes. It may cook up a little faster, so watch the oven.

Sprinkle lightly with Parmesan cheese, then defrosted peas. Place under broiler until chicken is crisp. Watch to prevent burning!

Delicious! A complete meal in one pan.

/ QUICK AND EASY CRANBERRY-ONION CHICKEN

Tasty and tangy.

SERVES 4-6   PREHEAT OVEN TO 350 DEGREES

- 1 whole chicken, cut up
- 1 12 ounce jar apricot preserves
- 1 14 ounce can whole cranberry sauce
- 1 16 ounce bottle of French dressing
- 1 dry packet Lipton's Onion Soup Mix

Spray a 9 x 13 pan with non-stick cooking spray. Combine the preserves, cranberry sauce, dressing and soup mix. Stir well to combine. Place chicken on prepared pan and pour dressing mixture over the chicken. Bake in a preheated 350 degree oven for about an hour. Baste occasionally with the mixture in the pan.

I serve it with fingerling potatoes that have been roasted.

P.S. you can use fat-free dressing and sugar free preserves

/ DIET VEGGIE STEW

4	cloves garlic, minced
2-3	tablespoons olive oil
1	onion, sliced
1-2	teaspoons beef flavoring (optional)
1	green pepper, diced
4	red potatoes, cubed skin on
½	cup long grain rice (not instant)
1	cup green cabbage, shredded
1	can red kidney beans
1	can diced tomatoes, do not drain
4	cups vegetable broth (low sodium)
2	tablespoons chili powder

In a large pot, sauté the garlic and onion in olive oil with beef seasoning until browned. Add the remaining ingredients. Boil, then reduce to a simmer over low heat for 2 hours. Stir occasionally.

/CASHEW CRUSTED SALMON

I am sure you will go "nuts" for this fish!

SERVES 4

- 2 **pounds of salmon**
- ¾ **cup chopped cashews**
- ½ **cup dry onion flakes**
  salt and pepper, to taste
- 2 **tablespoons olive oil**

Coat fish with a small amount of olive oil. Dip the salmon in the chopped cashews and onion flakes. Sprinkle pepper. If cashews have no salt on them, sprinkle salt on the fish.

Heat the olive oil in a saucepan and fry the coated salmon cashew side down. Cook each side for 4 minutes. Sprinkle cashews on fish if they fall off in the frying pan after it is cooked.

/GARY'S POACHED SALMON

On my third date with Gary Solomon, he surprised me with dinner at his house. He had flowers and candles on the table and made this delicious poached salmon. I was truly impressed and delighted with his efforts!

PREHEAT OVEN TO 350 DEGREES

1 **pound salmon, skin off**
1 **large lemon, sliced**
2 **tablespoons butter**
1 **tablespoon dill, fresh or dry**
   salt and pepper to taste
   cucumber sauce, optional

Season the fish with salt and pepper. Slice the lemon and place the slices over the whole fish. Put 1 tablespoon of butter on each side of the pan so its next to the fish, but not in the fish. Sprinkle the dill on the butter.

Bake in the 350 degree oven for about 25 minutes. Place on a platter and drizzle with the butter and dill "sauce". If you would like a little more citrus, squeeze a little more lemon over the fish.

P.S. Use the EASY CUCUMBER SAUCE recipe on the side.

ADRIENNE LANDAU'S HUNGARIAN GOULASH

Adrienne Landau was one of the stars of the fur industry. Adrienne says "this dish always brings out the gypsy in me. Every time I have this dish, it takes me back to my childhood when my grandfather and mother used to make it. Then we'd top it off with a dessert of chocolate eclairs!"

SERVES 4

- 2 tablespoons chicken fat
- 4 onions, chopped
- ½ green pepper, chopped dash of salt
- 3 cloves garlic
- 2 tablespoons Hungarian paprika
- 2 pound beef cubes, trimmed
- ½ cup water
- 1 chicken bouillon cube
- 1 bag fresh sauerkraut
- 1-2 cups sour cream

Grease bottom of a stew pot with chicken fat. Sauté chopped onions until clear. Add green pepper and salt. Add garlic and enough paprika to make the color a true red.

Add beef cubes and water. Keep stirring to blend. Add chicken cube, stir to dissolve and simmer for 15 minutes. Continue to add small amounts of water at intervals while simmering.

Rinse sauerkraut with cold water and add to beef mixture. Allow to simmer for 1½ - 2 hours until tender. Stir occasionally. Add a little more water if needed for gravy consistency.

Before serving, mix in sour cream to taste! This is delicious served with boiled potatoes or on a bed of broad egg noodles.

/MEAT LOAF

This is a cozy meat loaf that no one could refuse! Serve it with my fingerling potatoes and a green veggie of your choice.

PREHEAT OVEN TO 350 DEGREES

1 pound ground round beef
1 egg
3 tablespoons breadcrumbs
¼ teaspoon Lawry's Seasoned Salt
⅓ cup green pepper, chopped
⅓ cup red pepper, chopped
⅓ cup yellow pepper, chopped
½ cup chopped onions, optional
½ cup chopped mushrooms, optional
½ jar Heinz Chili Sauce
4 tablespoons brown sugar

Spray a loaf pan with non-stick cooking spray.

In a large bowl, mix the beef with an egg, the breadcrumbs and Lawry's. Add the chopped vegetables and form the mixture into a loaf. Place in pan and adjust size. Top with brown sugar and the chili sauce. Bake for 1 hour in a preheated 350 degree oven.

MICROWAVE FISH

I always use Lake Superior white fish

    2   pounds Lake Superior white fish, boned and cut in half
        Lawry's Seasoned Salt to taste
        pepper to taste
    ¼   cup milk
    ½   bottle chili sauce
    1   orange sliced

Spray a microwave baking pan with non-stick cooking spray. Place fish in pan with skin side down. Season with pepper and Lawry's Seasoned Salt. Mix milk with chili sauce and pour over fish. Place sliced orange around the fish (The milk will cut the fish smell in your kitchen). Cook on high for 8½ minutes and serve immediately.

*P.S. You can also bake in a 350 degree oven for
30-45 minutes or until cooked through.*

MICROWAVE MEAT LOAF

SERVES 4 - 6

        2   pounds chopped meat
        1   egg
        2   tablespoons seasoned bread crumbs
            Lawry's salt to taste
            pepper to taste
            garlic powder to taste
        2   tablespoons milk
        ½   bottle chili sauce
        2   rounded tablespoons brown sugar

Spray microwaveable loaf pans with non-stick cooking spray.

Mix chopped meat with egg, bread crumbs and seasonings and milk.

Form meat into a rectangular shape and place into loaf pan. Cover top with chili sauce and brown sugar. Cover with wax paper and cook on high for 10 minutes. Make sure meat is browned and cooked through.

GRANDMA FRAN'S
MEAT, PRUNES AND POTATOES

This is an old Russian family recipe. My mother-in-law makes this for every holiday and calls it "Flaumen and Potatoes". It's always a favorite...especially with the men.

5 pounds chuck roast
5 pounds potatoes
1 box prunes
½ cup brown sugar
½ bottle chili sauce
1 large onion, sliced
½ 8 ounce jar grape jelly
2 bunches carrots, cut into large pieces

Put all ingredients in a large pot. Cover and simmer for about 3 hours on top of stove on low heat. Stir occasionally.

Spray a large oven pan with non-stick cooking spray and pour in the entire stew. Place in a 300 degree oven for another 3 hours or until meat is very tender – falling off the fork.

You have a complete meal in one dish!

/OVEN-TO-FREEZER SPINACH LASAGNA

- 1 pound ground turkey or lean beef
- 3 garlic cloves, minced
- 2 10 ounce packages of frozen chopped spinach
- 2 jars (28 ounce) tomato sauce
- 1 15 ounce container ricotta or cottage cheese
- 2 large eggs, beaten
- 1 tablespoon oregano
- 1 tablespoon dried basil
- 1 teaspoon salt
- 1 16 ounce box no boil lasagna noodles
- 2 cups shredded mozzarella cheese
- 1 8 ounce can mushrooms, drained
  Parmesan cheese, grated

Line a 9 x 13 pan with foil long enough to create a tented cover.

Brown meat with garlic and drain the excess liquids. Thaw spinach and squeeze the water out. Mix spinach with tomato sauce, ricotta, beaten eggs, oregano, basil and salt. Spread thin layer of the sauce mixture in the prepared pan. Top with uncooked noodles and add sauce on top with 1 cup of mozzarella. Then add another layer of noodles, sauce, and top with 1 more cup of mozzarella. Top the lasagna with a thin layer of Parmesan cheese.

Cover the pan with the tented foil. Bake 50-60 minutes in a preheated 350 degree oven. Uncover the top and let cheese slightly brown about 5 minutes.

Freezes well.

JUDITH LEIBER'S TRANSYLVANIAN GULYA'S

Designer Judith Leiber is famous for her fabulous purses and belts. Her jeweled style is renown in the world of fashion. This recipe is a real "gem" too!

- 4 pounds sauerkraut
- ¼ pound margarine
- 4 large white onions, minced
- 2 tablespoons tomato paste
- 2 bouillon cubes paprika to taste
- 1½ pounds pork cut into ¾" cubes and salted
- 2 sticks Hungarian cooking sausage or Polish Kilbasza or Kosher frankfurters
- 1 large container sour cream
- ½ pound mushrooms
- 2 green peppers

Wash sauerkraut, drain in colander. Put in large pot without water. Cook on slow heat for 1½ hours, checking occasionally and adding a little water only if needed.

Melt margarine in large pan. Add minced onions and simmer tightly covered until wilted, for about 20 minutes. Add paprika, tomato paste and bouillon cubes. Add cut up pork. When done, mix with sauerkraut adding the rounds of sausage and ½ of the sour cream, mushrooms, and 1 green pepper, chopped. Cook 1 hour longer.

This dish is better cooled, refrigerated and warmed up the next day. When ready to serve, mix the other half of the sour cream and garnish with rounds of green pepper.

ISAAC MIZRAHI'S "YEBRA" AND PRUNE BUTTER SAUCE

Middle Eastern Stuffed Grape Leaves with Dried Apricots

Isaac Mizrahi has been an important contemporary designer. for decades. His innovative fashions are staples on the American fashion scene.

This recipe is an example of the complicated dishes he likes to prepare and loves to eat. It was one of his grandmother's specialties. When he was a boy he used to peel off the grape leaves and just eat the filling, which annoyed her immensely. Since he's grown up he's acquired a passionate taste for the complete dish which he and his mother often make.

1	small jar grape leaves
⅔	cup white rice, short grain
1	tablespoon vegetable oil
1	teaspoon cinnamon
1	teaspoon allspice
1	teaspoon salt
1	pound ground beef or veal
½	cup water
15	dried apricot halves

Carefully remove grape leaves from jar and rinse in bowl of cold water. Wash rice and in large bowl combine with vegetable oil, cinnamon, allspice and salt. Add ground beef and water. Mix thoroughly with hands. Mixture should be soft.

Taking one grape leaf at a time, remove stem (if any) with sharp knife. At base of leaf, place meat/rice mixture horizontally in long mound, not quite to edges of leaf, and roll carefully and tightly, folding in side to completely enclose mixture. Finished yebra should look like a cigar.

Place finished "cigars" in roaster and cover with prune butter sauce (recipe below), topping with apricot halves. Put aluminum foil directly on top of grape leaves and weigh down with glass or oven proof plate.

ISAAC MIZRAHI'S "YEBRA" AND PRUNE BUTTER SAUCE, cont.

Cook on stove top for 10 minutes, medium flame. Cover with lid and bake in pre-heated 350 degree oven for at least 2 hours. Add a little more water if all liquid evaporates when baking.

Prune Butter Sauce:
- 1 jar prune butter
- 1 jar full of lemon juice
- ⅓ cup sugar
- 2 cups water

In a sauce pan add prune butter. Refill same jar with lemon juice and stir in, along with sugar. Cook over medium flame for 10 – 15 minutes.

Using ½ of sauce, dilute with 2 cups water. Pour over stuffed grape leaves. Remaining sauce may be stored in refrigerator for several months.

ALBERT AND PEARL NIPON'S BRISKET WITH KASHA AND BOWTIES

Albert and Pearl Nipon have been a top name in dress designing for many years. These recipes were originally from Pearl's grandmother. They have always been family favorites, served as a complete meal with applesauce and coleslaw.

SERVES 6   PREHEAT OVEN TO 450 DEGREES

Brisket:

- 3 pounds brisket, first cut
- salt and pepper to taste
- garlic powder to taste
- Lawry's Seasoned Salt to taste
- 1 package Goodman's Onion Soup

Kasha:

- 1 package whole grain groats
- 1 egg
- salt and pepper
- 2 cups hot water
- 1 pound bowtie pasta

. . . .

Season meat with salt, pepper, garlic powder and Lawry's Seasoned Salt. Roast in a preheated 450 degree oven for 15 minutes. Turn over and continue browning for an additional 15 minutes.

Dilute onion soup with amount of water called for on package (more water might be added if more gravy is desired). Add it to roasting pan and cover with heavy duty tin foil. Reduce oven temperature to 425 degrees and continue cooking for an additional 2 hours or until fork comes out of meat easily.

To prepare groats: mix whole grain groats with egg, salt and pepper in shallow pan. Cook over low heat until dry. Add hot water, cover and allow to simmer on low flame until water is absorbed and groats are tender (check package).

ALBERT AND PEARL NIPON'S BRISKET WITH KASHA AND BOWTIES, cont.

Boil bow ties as directed on package. Drain and mix with cooked groats. Add a little gravy from brisket. Slice brisket thin and serve with groats and bowtie mixture (Kasha) as a wonderful side dish.

SHRIMP CREOLE

Every time I had to impress and entertain at the same time, this recipe was always a winner.

SERVES 4-6

- 3 tablespoons vegetable oil
- ½ cup chopped onions
- ½ cup chopped celery
- 1 clove garlic, minced
- 2 cups canned tomatoes
- 1 8 ounce can tomato sauce
- 1½ teaspoons salt
- 1 teaspoon sugar
- ½ teaspoon chili powder (optional ½ teaspoon more if you like it a little hotter)
- 1 tablespoon Worcestershire sauce
- ¼ teaspoon Tabasco sauce
- 1 teaspoon cornstarch
- 2 teaspoons water
- 1 pound raw, cleaned shrimps
- ½ cup chopped green pepper

In a large pan cook onion, celery and garlic in hot oil until tender but not brown. Add tomatoes, tomato sauce, salt, sugar, chili powder, Worcestershire sauce and Tabasco. Cook over low heat for 35 minutes uncovered.

Mix cornstarch with water and stir into the sauce mixture. Cook until sauce thickens.

Add shrimp and green pepper. Cover and cook for about 5 minutes until shrimp is cooked through, but green pepper is still crunchy.

I serve this around a rice ring filled with Le Sueur peas.

MARIA RODRIGUEZ' HUCHINANGO ALA PUERTO VALLARTA

Puerto Vallarta Style Red Snapper

Maria Rodriguez brought stardom to the Chicago fashion industry. Not only does she weave magic into her unique fabrics, but her designs have placed her in a class by herself. Maria got this recipe from friends who own the "Marisol – No. 11" restaurant in the old market place in Puerto Vallarta. This dish is a favorite of Maria's, and her husband, Brad Cole.

Seasoned Dressing (to be prepared three days in advance)

- ⅔ **cup garlic, minced**
- ⅓ **cup parsley, minced**
- 4 **bay leaves, crushed**
- 1 **teaspoon black pepper vinegar pure virgin olive oil**

....

Place all spices in a one litre jar and fill 60% with vinegar and 40% olive oil, Let stand 3 days.

(This dressing may stored and used all summer long when you grill shrimp, orange roughy, or similar whole fish)

Preparation:

4 whole fresh red snappers (approximately 1 – 2 pounds each)

Diagonally slit fish in 5 areas. Sea salt and flour the entire fish. Grill on one side, turn over and spoon ample amount of the above dressing on fish. Repeat on reverse side. Regrill first side and add more dressing. (Note: for red snapper, allow a total of 10 minutes of grilling time per 1 inch for thickness.)

When properly grilled, the bones of red snapper should easily separate from fish.

Serve with Spanish rice mixed with peas and chopped carrots, refried pinto beans, a side of lettuce, tomatoes, black olives and warmed fresh corn tortillas.

THE BEST QUICHE LORRAINE

1   frozen pie crust, defrosted
½   cup butter
1   cup onions, chopped
1   cup mushrooms, chopped (fresh or canned)
½   cup Swiss cheese, grated
1   tablespoon flour
3   eggs
¾   cup half and half cream
1   teaspoon salt
⅛   teaspoon pepper

In a large skillet, melt butter and sauté onions and mushrooms. Onions should be translucent. Place onions and mushrooms on bottom of pie crust.

Mix grated Swiss with flour. Sprinkle cheese mixture over onions and mushrooms.

Beat eggs with half and half. Add salt and pepper and stir well. Pour over cheese.

Bake in a preheated 375 degree oven for 40 minutes.

Cool slightly before slicing and serving.

Optional additions (substituted for onions and mushrooms):
green pepper, tomatoes, asparagus, broccoli, ham*, salami*

*These ingredients do not have to be sautéed.

DONNA KARAN'S CRISPY DIJON CHICKEN

Donna Karan creates the most outstanding clothing for the "woman on the go... who has a very busy life style!" Her sophisticated line appears under her own label and also DKNY. Her sophisticated clothes are easy to wear and great for travel. This recipe is one of Donna's favorites! She suggests serving it hot with an asparagus salad, or it's great to serve for a picnic with a big salad and lots of whole grained Italian bread, grilled with herbs and pureed olive spread.

- 1 free-range chicken, cut into 8 pieces
  garlic flavored oil
  fresh ground pepper
- ½ cup white wine
- ⅓ cup Dijon mustard
- 1 cup crushed whole grain cereal flakes

Place chicken pieces in broiling or roasting pan with low sides. Brush pieces lightly with garlic oil. Sprinkle with fresh ground pepper to taste.

Broil chicken, skin side down until opaque and beginning to brown. Turn chicken over and repeat.

Mix wine and mustard to make marinade. Brush mixture on chicken and sprinkle generously with cereal flakes, Broil chicken again until crispy and brown. Repeat on other side.

Turn oven to bake and reduce temperature to 350 degrees. Continue to cook chicken for 10 minutes.

Serve hot or warm.

JOAN'S CARROT BREAD-CAKE

I make this recipe every time I do a holiday dinner!

PREHEAT OVEN TO 350 DEGREES

- ½ cup sweet butter
- 1 stick margarine
- ¾ cup brown sugar
- 1 cup grated carrots
- ½ teaspoon salt
- ½ teaspoon baking soda
- 2 eggs
- 1½ cups flour
- 1 teaspoon baking powder
- 1 tablespoon water
- 1 tablespoon lemon juice

Melt butter and margarine in a small saucepan. Mix all the rest of the ingredients together in a large bowl. Add melted butter and margarine. Pour mixture into a small tube shaped jello mold that is sprayed with non-stick cooking spray. Bake in a preheated 350 degree oven for 45 minutes.

This recipe serves approximately 10 people. Cut small pieces because this is a very rich side dish!

BECKY BISOULIS' GREEK CHICKEN

Winner of the Chicago Gold Coast Award for the best new designer, Becky Bisoulis' designs were easy to wear and beautiful to look at. Whether in satins, lace and pearls or simple cotton, Ms. Bisoulis' designs were all winners and so is this delicious chicken! Becky said, "If guests are Irish or Greek, allow one large potato per person, otherwise one small one will do."

SERVES 8   PREHEAT OVEN TO 375 DEGREES

- 3   medium whole chickens
- 8   Idaho potatoes*
- ½   cup olive oil
- ¾   cup butter
- 3   lemons, cut into wedges
      salt and pepper to taste
      lots and lots of oregano
- ⅓   cup Newman's Sun Dried Tomato Dressing or other tomato marinade

. . . .

1. Place scrubbed potatoes with skins on in the oven at 375 degrees and bake for 45 minutes.
2. While potatoes are baking, clean chickens and place in a large baking pan (Pan should be large enough for the potatoes, also).
3. Sprinkle chickens with olive oil and place chunks of butter inside and outside of chickens.
4. Squeeze the lemon wedges all over and leave some wedges inside the chickens and in the pan.
5. Sprinkle with salt and pepper to taste. Add liberal amounts of oregano inside and all over the chickens.
6. Reduce oven temperature to 325 degrees.

cont.

7. When potatoes are baked, remove from oven and slice about 1½ inches thick. Place them around chickens. There should be a nice amount of juice from chickens so you will be immersing potatoes into liquid.

8. About ½ hour before chickens are done (you will know doneness when chicken leg lifts easily from the joint and the skin is crispy brown) sprinkle ⅓ cup tomato marinade all over.

P.S. Add pan juices to each serving. Becky served huge chunks of Greek bread, slightly toasted, to dip into the juices.

ARNOLD SCAASI'S CARIBBEAN CHICKEN

Arnold Scaasi's elegant, entrance-making gowns have made him a sought after designer, Barbara Bush chose him to create her inaugural gown. Arnold says of this recipe, "In the country, we use fresh farm chickens and double or triple this recipe for guests. In the city, it's dinner for four in my small dining room with its very large Dubuffet painting. I like the contrast of a simple, but flavorful dish, with a formal, beautifully set table and great art."

SERVES 4

- 1 chicken, quartered flour salt and pepper
- 2 tablespoons margarine
- 6 medium potatoes, peeled and quartered
- 6 large carrots, sliced, about ½ inch thick
- 1 medium yellow onion, chopped
- 2 10 ounce cans chicken broth
- ½ cup white wine
  dash of Tabasco sauce

Dust chicken lightly with flour and season with salt and pepper. Brown chicken in skillet on both sides in margarine (for 15 minutes), drain off fat. In separate pot, with boiling water, cook potatoes and carrots for ½ hour. Sauté onions in separate deep skillet and add chicken broth, wine, salt, pepper and Tabasco to taste. Add chicken and bring to a boil. Reduce heat and simmer slowly. Drain potatoes and carrots and add to large skillet with chicken and balance of ingredients. Simmer for approximately 1 hour and 15 minutes on low flame.

✎ CHICKEN SCHNITZEL

I got this recipe from my daughter-in-law Hadas. It is so easy to prepare and so delicious to eat. I sometimes use PANKO, which is Japanese Bread Crumbs. They have a little more crunch to their texture. Either way, this is sure to be a hit with your family and friends! Kids love this delicious, nutritious chicken.

- 2 **pounds of boneless chicken breast**
- 2 **cups of bread crumbs (can be seasoned)**
- 2 **eggs**
  - **canola oil**
  - **salt & pepper**
  - **sesame seeds (optional)**

Pour a generous amount of canola oil onto the frying pan and begin to heat.

In a shallow bowl, lightly beat the eggs with a fork. Pour the bread crumbs into a separate shallow bowl.

Dip on chicken breast at a time into the eggs and then into the bread crumbs. Flip chicken piece to the opposite side so that both sides are covered in bread crumbs.

When the oil is bubbling hot, place the chicken pieces with bread crumbs into the frying pan. Then sprinkle with salt, pepper (and sesame seeds if desired). Watch carefully. After approximately 5-7 minutes, flip chicken piece to cook on the other side. Cook until edges begin to turn brown. Place chicken on paper towels to drain and cool.

GRANDMA FRAN'S CHEESE PANCAKES

This recipe is always a favorite! My mother-in-law always had cottage cheese in her refrigerator for a last-minute meal.

YIELD: 8 MEDIUM PANCAKES

- 1 pound large or small curd cottage cheese
- 2 eggs
- ¾-1 cup flour
  vegetable oil (for frying)
  sour cream
  -and/or-
  sugar (for topping)

. . . .

In a medium size bowl, mix cottage cheese with eggs. Add flour, a little at a time, until the consistency is like a pancake batter.

Using a large frying pan, cover the bottom with vegetable oil. Heat oil over medium temperature. When oil is hot, scoop large spoonfuls of batter into the pan. Turn once when golden brown. Drain on paper towels.

Serve with sour cream and sugar if desired. This is great with my egg salad or tuna salad.

This recipe can be doubled!

GLAZED CHICKEN

This recipe is easy and delicious. I serve it with my mushroom rice ring.

1   whole chicken, cut up
    Lawry's Seasoned Salt to taste
1   bottle Milani's 1890 French Salad Dressing
1   12 ounce jar apricot preserves

Spray a 9 x 13 pan with non-stick cooking spray.

Season chicken with Lawry's Seasoned Salt and place skin side down in prepared pan. Broil until browned, then turn over and continue to broil until chicken is crispy. Combine dressing with preserves and pour over chicken.

Turn oven to 350 degrees and bake for an additional 30 – 45 minutes.

TERIYAKI GLAZED SALMON

I love the way the honey and teriyaki sauce coat the salmon. The flavor is wonderful over rice.

- 1 **pound salmon, skin off**
- 3 **tablespoons honey**
- 5 **tablespoons teriyaki sauce**
- 1 **tablespoon light brown sugar**
  salt and pepper to taste

Mix together the honey, teriyaki sauce and brown sugar. Sprinkle salt and pepper on the fish. Pour the sauce mixture over the fish.

Bake in a 9 x 13 pan for about 20 minutes. After 10 minutes spoon the glaze from the pan over the fish and continue to bake. It will have a delicious, tangy taste.

P.S. I spray the pan so clean up is easy.

/VEGGIE TURKEY BURGERS

YIELD: 4 BURGERS

- **1 pound ground turkey**
- **½ cup green pepper, roughly chopped**
- **½ cup red pepper, roughly chopped**
- **½ cup yellow pepper, roughly chopped**
- **½ cup mushrooms, roughly chopped**
- **½ cup onions, roughly chopped**
- **½ teaspoon Lawry's seasoning**

Combine all ingredients in a large bowl. Form the mixture into burger patties. I love using a grill pan to cook, but you can also bake or grill them outdoors. Make sure to cook each side through.

Be lazy and get all your veggies at your favorite salad bar!

MUSHROOM RICE RING

1   pound rice (I use Uncle Ben's)
1   pint mushrooms, washed and sliced
1   can water chestnuts, sliced
¼   cup chopped green pepper or sliced pea pods
1   packet of beef bouillon
1   scrambled egg

Cook rice according to directions on package. Add all vegetables and stir in bouillon. Mix well.

Scramble an egg and add to rice mixture. Stir well to combine.

Spray a 6 cup ring mold with non-stick cooking spray and pat down rice mixture. Put in oven to keep warm until needed or refrigerate and then heat before serving.

*P.S. You can use baby peas or baby carrots glazed with
brown sugar and butter in center of mold.*

/NOT YOUR MAMA'S STRING BEAN CASSEROLE

PREHEAT OVEN TO 350 DEGREES

1¼ pounds string beans
 2 tablespoons butter
 2 tablespoons chopped onions
 ½ cup mushrooms
 2 tablespoons flour
 ½ cup sour cream
 2 cups mozzarella cheese
 2 cups cornflakes
 2 tablespoons butter, cut into small pieces

Spray a Pyrex or metal pan with non-stick cooking spray.

Cut green beans in half and sauté in 2 tablespoons butter. Add onions. Then add the mushrooms, flour, salt and pepper to taste. Remove from heat and add sour cream. Place in the prepared dish.

Cover the green bean mixture with mozzarella cheese and top with cornflakes. Dot the top of the casserole with bits of butter.

Bake for 25 minutes and serve.

SPINACH NOODLE CASSEROLE

- ½ pound fine egg noodles, cooked and drained
- 1 cup cottage cheese
- 1 cup sour cream
-    dash onion powder
-    dash garlic salt
- 1 tablespoon Worcestershire sauce
- ½ cup Parmesan cheese, grated
- 2 packages frozen Stouffer's Spinach Souffle, defrosted

Mix together cottage cheese, sour cream, dash of onion powder and dash of garlic salt, Worcestershire sauce and Parmesan cheese. Add cooked and drained noodles and stir to coat.

Pour the noodle mixture into a greased 9 x 13 glass dish. Spread spinach soufflé over top of noodles. Bake in a preheated 350 degree oven for 40 minutes. Cool slightly and spoon out individual servings or cut into squares. This recipe may be prepared in advance and frozen.

/ SQUASH CASSEROLE

This is my daughter-in-law Hadas' easy and delish recipe. This was a girl who didn't know how to cook when she married my son. Boy did she fool me!!

PREHEAT OVEN TO 350 DEGREES

- 1   12 ounce box of frozen cooked squash
- ½   stick margarine, melted
- 2   cups coffee creamer (can be non-diary)
- 3   eggs
- 1   cup sugar
- 1   cup flour
     cinnamon to garnish (optional)

Put all ingredients together in a blender and pour the mixture into a 8 inch square glass pan sprayed with non-stick cooking spray. Bake in a preheated 350 degree oven for 1 hour. Sprinkle cinnamon on top before baking it if you desire.

/CRISPY ROASTED FINGERLING POTATOES

fingerling potatoes
olive oil
salt and pepper
minced garlic (optional)
Parmesan cheese (optional)

In a large bowl, toss potatoes with enough olive oil to coat the potatoes completely. Toss with salt and pepper and bake in a 9 x 13 pan. Bake in the preheated 425 degree oven about 30 minutes or until brown and crispy.

I use the same method for other veggies like broccoli, cauliflower, beets, and Brussels sprouts, cut into bite sized pieces.

KIESELSTEIN-CORD'S SWEET POTATO BASKETS

Barry Kieselstein-Cord is a Coty award winning jewelry designer. His belts, ear-rings and accessories are all considered pieces of art. CeCe Cord handles the art of cooking with the same degree of success! This recipe originally appeared in **The New York Times Magazine.** *It's a delicious side dish!*

SERVES 6

- 3 oranges
- 6 sweet potatoes
- 3 tablespoons butter
- 2 tablespoons brown sugar
- ½ cup pecans, chopped
- 3 ounces bourbon
- 1 package mini-marshmallows

1. Cut oranges in half and remove sections with grapefruit knife and spoon (save sections for breakfast or dessert).
2. Scallop edges of oranges with paring knife and set aside.
3. Pare potatoes, place in saucepan, cover with water and cook until tender.
4. Drain potatoes, put through ricer or mash with a potato masher. Beat in butter, sugar, pecans and bourbon. Mix well.
5. Fill orange shells with mashed potato mixture. Top with marshmallows.
6. Just before serving, place in oven to reheat, then place under broiler until marshmallows are just browned.

NEVER FROWN BRISKET

When most people hear brisket is being served, they usually make a sad face remembering their mother's brisket being greasy, fatty, stringy, or tough to chew. This recipe is a favorite for all generations!

- 6 **pounds brisket, first cut**
  Lawry's Seasoned Salt
- 1 **clove fresh garlic, minced**
- 1 **small jar Heinz chili sauce**
- 4 **tablespoons brown sugar**

I make sure that there is almost no fat on my brisket, so I have to trim it myself after the butcher gets finished trimming.

1. Place meat in a shallow pan and sprinkle meat with seasoned salt on both sides.
2. Sprinkle minced garlic over one side of brisket and broil until top is brown, about 5 minutes. Turn over and repeat.
3. Turn over to original side and pour chili sauce over whole brisket. Fill empty chili jar ¾'s full of water and pour into shallow pan around the brisket.
4. Sprinkle brown sugar on top of chili sauce that is on top of brisket.
5. Cover tightly with foil paper and turn oven to 325 degrees and cook for 1½ hours.
6. Turn oven up to 350 degrees and continue cooking for an additional 1½ hours or until a fork comes out of meat easily.
7. Remove the excess liquid, scrape off brown sugar coating and put into a bowl in refrigerator to use later as gravy.
8. Slice brisket with an electric knife or take it to the butcher for a more professional job.
9. Pour gravy over brisket and heat in oven until warm, approximately 20 – 25 minutes.

SANDRA ROTH'S CARROT SOUFFLÉ

Sandra is a well-known sportswear designer. Her CIAOSPORT label is a fashion favorite. Her soufflé is sure to become a favorite, too.

SERVES 8   PREHEAT OVEN TO 350 DEGREES

- ¾ butter
- ¾ cup light shortening
- 1 cup dark brown sugar
- 2 cups flour
- 1 teaspoon baking soda
- 1 teaspoon salt
- 2 teaspoons baking powder
- 4 egg yolks
- 2 teaspoons lemon juice
- 2 tablespoons water
- 3 cups carrots, grated
- 5 egg whites

1. Cream butter and add shortening and sugar.
2. In separate bowl, mix flour, baking soda, salt and baking powder. Set aside.
3. Beat egg yolks until light in color. Add lemon juice, water and carrots.
4. Add flour mixture to butter mixture. Blend well. Add carrots.
5. In a separate bowl, beat egg whites until stiff. Fold egg whites into carrot mixture.
6. Pour into a greased 8 inch round casserole or soufflé dish and bake for 1 hour and 10 minutes in a preheated 350 degree oven.
7. Test with a knife in the center. The knife must come out clean and dry.

AUNT LYLA'S KUGEL

I have eaten many noodle kugels in my time, but this is my favorite.

SERVES 24   PREHEAT OVEN TO 350 DEGREES

- 1   pound broad egg noodles, cooked and drained
- 4   eggs, lightly beaten
- ½   cup sugar
- 1   pound cottage cheese
- 1   20 ounce can crushed pineapple, drained well
- 1   8 ounce jar apricot preserves
- 1   cup corn flakes, crushed (or less)
- ½   pound butter, melted
- 1   tablespoon sugar (for garnish)

Mix cooked noodles with eggs, sugar, cottage cheese, pineapple and preserves. Put mixture in a 9 x 13 pan sprayed with non-stick cooking spray. Cover mixture with crushed corn flakes and drizzle with melted butter. Sprinkle a little sugar over butter and bake in a preheated 350 degree oven for 1½ hours or until top is browned.

Cool slightly and cut into squares and serve.

This recipe freezes beautifully!

HOT OR COLD SALMON LOAF

I serve this when I make a dairy lunch.

PREHEAT OVEN TO 350 DEGREES

- 1 **cup salmon or tuna, drained**
- 2 **cups plain bread crumbs**
- ½ **cup milk**
- 1 **egg, well beaten**
- 1 **teaspoon salt**
- 1 **tablespoon parsley, finely chopped**
  dash of pepper
- 2 **tablespoons butter, melted**
- 1 **tablespoon lemon juice**

Flake fish and remove any bones. Add all ingredients together and mix well. Pour into a 8½ or 9 inch loaf pan sprayed with non-stick cooking spray. Set pan into another pan partially filled with water and bake in a preheated 350 degree oven for 40 minutes or until firm. Unmold and slice, or if serving cold, refrigerate for a few hours before serving.

This recipe can be prepared in advance and then frozen. Use the Easy Cucumber Sauce on the side.

MAGGIE'S MIXED UP VEGGIE CASSEROLE

This is a great side dish for a picnic or a family gathering. It's easy to make and delicious to eat!

PREHEAT OVEN TO 350 DEGREES

- 2 packages frozen chopped broccoli, thaw and drain well
- 2 large cans cream style corn
- 2 tablespoons chopped onion
- 2 eggs (or egg whites) slightly beaten
- ½ stick margarine, melted
- 2 cups Pepperidge Farm Corn Bread stuffing
- ½ stick margarine, melted

Mix together broccoli, corn, onion, eggs and margarine and pour into a 9 x 13 casserole that has been sprayed with non-stick cooking spray. Spread vegetables out evenly to cover pan.

Sprinkle corn bread stuffing over vegetable mixture and drizzle with melted margarine.

Bake in a preheated 350 degree oven for 1 hour.

To serve, spoon out individual servings!

TIME FOR BREAKFAST

TIME FOR BREAKFAST

GOOD MORNING (OR ANYTIME) COFFEE!

I came up with this recipe before you could buy flavored coffee. It still works really well when company drops by.

For the best coffee you'll ever taste, sprinkle 1 teaspoon of cinnamon on top of ground coffee for 12 cups of coffee. Add 2 drops of vanilla extract and stir to blend.

For chocolaty flavor also add 1 teaspoon of unsweetened cocoa.

Brew and enjoy a cup of coffee sure to bring on the compliments.

GERMAN APPLE PANCAKE

- ¼ cup sugar
- ¼ cup brown sugar
- 1 teaspoon cinnamon
- 4 apples, sliced
- ¼ cup butter
- 2 eggs
- ½ cup flour
- ½ cup milk
- ½ teaspoon salt

Use a 8 or 9 inch round cake pan with non-stick cooking spray.

Combine sugar, brown sugar, and cinnamon and sprinkle bottom of pan. Lay apple slices on top of sugar and cinnamon so there are enough apple slices to cover the bottom of the pan. Cut butter into small pieces and dot the apples.

Bake in a preheated 350 degree oven for 10 minutes.

Meanwhile beat the eggs, flour, milk and salt together. Pour mixture on baked apples. Return to oven for an additional 15 minutes. Remove from oven and invert on plate. Serve immediately. Delish!

EGG SOUFFLÉ

PREHEAT OVEN TO 350 DEGREES

- 1 **small cream cheese**
- ½ **cup milk**
- 8 **eggs**
- 1 **tablespoon butter**
   salt & pepper to taste

Whip all ingredients together and pour into a 4 cup soufflé dish sprayed with non-stick cooking spray. Bake 20 minutes in a preheated 350 degree oven.

Serve immediately.

JUDY'S BRUNCH COFFEE CAKE

When I was staying in L.A. a few years ago, my very dear friend Judy Tallarico made brunch for us one morning and served this cake. We couldn't stop eating it.

PREHEAT OVEN TO 350 DEGREES

1	bag whole pecans
2	frozen Rhodes breads (2 loaves in package), defrosted
1	package butterscotch pudding and pie filling, not instant
½	cup brown sugar
1	teaspoon cinnamon
¼	pound butter, melted

1. Spray or grease a bundt pan and cover the bottom with the whole pecans.
2. Cut defrosted Rhodes Frozen Breads into large pieces. Drop bread chunks on nuts.
3. Sprinkle the box of pudding on top of bread.
4. Sprinkle brown sugar on top of pudding layer.
5. Sprinkle a teaspoon of cinnamon on top of the brown sugar.
6. Drizzle melted butter over the brown sugar.

Put in the refrigerator overnight. In the morning, take out of refrigerator 3 hours before baking to let the dough rise. Bake for ½ hour in a preheated 350 degree oven. Remove from oven and wait 10 minutes, then invert on a plate. This cake must be eaten immediately.

BLUEBERRY FRUIT CRUNCH

This is a quick, easy and delicious coffee cake.

PREHEAT OVEN TO 350 DEGREES

- 1 package Duncan Hines Blueberry Muffin mix
- ¼ cup butter
- 1 can (1 pound 5 ounces) fruit pie filling (choice of cherry, peach, apple, blueberry or pineapple)
- ½ teaspoon cinnamon
- ½ teaspoon almond extract
- ¼ cup chopped nuts – walnuts or pecans

In a small saucepan, melt butter and set aside to cool. Empty packaged blueberries into strainer and rinse under cold water. Set aside.

Pour fruit pie filling into an 8 or 9 inch square sprayed with non-stick cooking spray.

Combine cinnamon, almond extract and blueberries and sprinkle over pie filling. Add dry muffin mix and nuts to cool melted butter and combine with fork until crumbly. Distribute evenly over fruit in pan.

Bake in a preheated 350 degree oven for 30 – 40 minutes, until golden brown.

This cake is great served with ice cream or Cool Whip.

BANANA BREAD

When I first got married, 45 years ago, I made this recipe almost all the time. It's still a favorite today as a breakfast bread – or anytime!

PREHEAT OVEN TO 350 DEGREES

- ⅓ cup butter
- ½ cup sugar
- 2 eggs
- 1¾ cups sifted all purpose flour
- 1 teaspoon baking powder
- ½ teaspoon baking soda
- 1½ cups ripe bananas, mashed
- ½ cup chopped walnuts or pecans (optional)

Cream together butter and sugar; add eggs and beat well. Sift all dry ingredients together and add to creamed mixture on low speed. Blend in bananas and mix well. If desired, stir in nuts.

Pour into a well sprayed loaf pan (9½ x 5 x 3). Bake for 40 – 45 minutes in a preheated 350 degree oven or until a toothpick comes out clean.

Cool for 1 hour before removing from pan.

Freezes well.

GREAT BLUEBERRY BREAKFAST CAKE

Cake:

- ¼ cup butter
- ¾ cup sugar
- 1 egg
- ½ cup milk
- 2 cups flour
- 2 teaspoons baking powder
- 2 cups fresh blueberries (toss with some flour so berries won't sink)

Topping:

- ¼ cup butter
- ½ cup sugar
- ⅓ cup flour
- ½ teaspoon cinnamon

In a mixer, cream butter and sugar. Add egg and milk and mix well. Slowly add flour and baking powder. By hand, fold in floured blueberries. Pour batter into a greased 8 or 9 inch square pan.

Prepare topping by placing all the ingredients in a bowl and cutting with a pastry knife or fork to make a crumbly mixture. Sprinkle on top of batter and bake in a preheated 350 degree oven for 35 minutes.

Freezes well.

BREAKFAST BARS

I like these early in the morning, but they are wonderful any time of the day.

YIELD: 36 BARS   PREHEAT OVEN TO 350 DEGREES

- 1   8 ounce package of chopped pitted dates
- 1   cup raisins
- 1   cup walnuts or pecans, chopped
- 1   teaspoon grated orange peel (optional)
- 2   teaspoons cinnamon
- 1   cup sugar
- ¼   pound butter
- 1   teaspoon vanilla extract
- 2   eggs
- 2   cups all purpose flour
- 2   teaspoons baking powder
- 2   tablespoons orange juice
-     confectioners sugar to garnish

Grease 2 cookie sheets and set aside.

In a large bowl, mix together dates, raisins, walnuts and orange peel. Mix ½ cup sugar with the cinnamon. Pour over fruits and nuts and stir, making sure they are well coated. In a separate bowl, cream butter and remaining ½ cup of sugar and vanilla extract until light and fluffy. Beat in eggs, one at a time. Stir in flour, baking powder and orange juice. Add fruit and nut mixture and beat until well blended. The dough will be stiff.

Shape into logs, 2 on each cookie sheet. Bake 15 – 20 minutes in a preheated 350 degree oven until bars are light brown. They will seem soft, but will firm up as they cool. When cool, cut diagonally into ¾ inch bars. Sprinkle with confectioners sugar.

Freezes well.

DIET BRAN MUFFINS

YIELD: 4 MUFFINS   PREHEAT OVEN TO 350 DEGREES

- 8 tablespoons Millers Bran
- 3 tablespoons powdered skim milk
- ½ teaspoon cinnamon
- 1 packet of Sweet 'N Low or Equal
- 3 tablespoons water
- 1 egg
- ½ teaspoon vanilla extract
- 1 apple, sliced then cut into small chunks

In a small bowl combine by hand the bran, powdered milk, cinnamon and sugar substitute. Stir in water, egg and vanilla extract to moisten. DO NOT OVERBEAT. Add apples and stir just to cover.

Spray 4 muffin cups with non-stick cooking spray or line with paper cups. Fill them ½ full with batter and bake for 25 minutes in a preheated 350 degree oven.

These muffins are only good for one day. That's why I only make 4. But if you need more double this recipe.

RASPBERRY MELTAWAY MUFFINS

These muffins will melt in your mouth!

YIELD: 24 MINI MUFFINS   PREHEAT OVEN TO 350 DEGREES

- ¾ cup (1½ sticks) well chilled, unsalted butter
- ¼ cup sugar
- 1 tablespoon sour cream
- 1 teaspoon vanilla extract
- ¼ teaspoon salt (optional)
- 1½ cups flour
- ¼+ cup raspberry preserves
  confectioners sugar

Cream butter and sugar. Add sour cream, vanilla extract and salt. Mix until well blended. Add flour and blend well.

Take 1 tablespoon of dough and form small ball and press into mini muffin tins, sprayed with non-stick cooking spray. Bake in a preheated 350 degree oven for about 25 minutes.

Remove from oven and let cool 5 – 10 minutes. Remove from muffin tins and cover the top of each with ½ teaspoon of raspberry preserves. Place each into mini muffin papers. Dust with confectioners sugar.

This recipe freezes well.

BUFFET ACCESSORIES

BUFFET ACCESSORIES

CAROLYNE ROEHM'S OMELETTE SOUFFLÉ AU GRAND MARNIER

Carolyne Roehm got her start as an assistant to Oscar de la Renta. Now she stands firmly on her own two feet... but she's never caught standing around. Sophisticated and elegant women seek out her couture gowns and fabulous sportswear. This dessert is a light and refreshing way to end a special dinner.

SERVES 6   PREHEAT OVEN TO 400 DEGREES

- 6 individual omelette pans (copper is recommended)
- 6 egg yolks
- 7 egg whites
- 2 tablespoons super fine sugar
- ¼ cup English marmalade
- 10 tablespoons Grand Marnier
  confectioners sugar
- 6 candied violets, optional
- 6 mint sprigs, optional

Beat egg yolks with whisk until frothy. Add super fine sugar to taste. Blend in marmalade. Add 2-4 tablespoons Grand Marnier to taste. Whisk all ingredients, just to blend.

Dust omelette pans with super fine sugar. Place 1 tablespoon Grand Marnier in bottom of each. In a separate bowl, whip egg whites until stiff peaks begin to form. Gently, fold in yolk mixture, just until incorporated. Be careful not to break the egg whites. Mixture will be lumpy.

Carefully spoon into pans. Gently stir before each serving to keep ingredients properly combined. Bake in a preheated 400 degree oven for 6 minutes, or until golden on top. The edges will be lightly done and the inside will be moist.

To serve, dust with confectioners sugar and garnish with violet and mint sprig.

*Since the cooper pans are very hot, Carolyne suggests putting a pretty napkin on the serving plate to prevent from cracking.

GLAZED PARTY NUTS

These are my "famous" party nuts. I make them for all my dinner parties. This simple recipe is sure to impress your guests!

PREHEAT OVEN TO 325 DEGREES

- 2 **egg whites**
- 1 **cup sugar**
   pinch of salt
- 2 **pounds walnuts or pecans**

Beat egg whites into peaks while slowly adding sugar and salt. Carefully fold in nuts.

Spray cookie sheet with non-stick cooking spray. Spread sugar-glazed nuts in a single layer on the pan.

Bake in a preheated 325 degree oven for 20 minutes. Turn nuts and bake for an additional 20 minutes or until dry. Watch your oven, they may not need all that time.

Cool completely and place in an airtight container. They will keep fresh for weeks!

P.S. If you want a cinnamon-flavored nut, just add teaspoon of cinnamon to the egg and sugar mixture.

ANN LAWRENCE'S DAVINITY

Ann Lawrence is truly a "divine" designer. She creates wonderful dresses and gowns for those special, enchanted evenings. This recipe for a white candy, similar to fudge was handed down to her by her family who were bakers and candy makers in Arizona.

- 2 cups sugar
- ½ cup water
- ½ cup white corn syrup
- 2 egg whites
- ¼ cup cherries, drained (optional)
- 3 tablespoons lemon extract
- ¾ cup almonds, blanched

In a saucepan, heat sugar, water and corn syrup, watching carefully while stirring. Bring to a boil (do not scorch). Beat egg whites until dry. Then pour sugar mixture into egg whites while continuing to beat. Beat until fairly dry, white and fluffy. Add cherries (optional), lemon extract and almonds. Stir.

Pour onto a greased pan or wax paper lined platter.

Cut into squares when candy has set. Eat and enjoy.

CHOCOLATE CARAMEL MATZO

This is a recipe that I make for Passover. It is always a hit as it combines the salty and the sweet and has a delicious crunch. It's a great holiday treat!

PREHEAT OVEN TO 350 DEGREES

- 2 sheets matzo; or enough to cover a jelly roll pan
- 1 cup butter
- 1 cup light brown sugar
- 1 12 ounce package semi-sweet chocolate chips
  chopped pecans or walnuts (optional)

Line a jelly roll pan with parchment paper.

Using full sheets of matzo, cover the entire pan in a single layer. (You may need to break off pieces of another matzo to cover the whole pan).

Melt the butter and brown sugar in a saucepan until the mixture is bubbly. Pour over the matzo and bake about 10 minutes. Cool. Melt chocolate chips and drizzle the chocolate across the matzo. Spread to cover the caramel layer. Sprinkle nuts on top of the matzo. Cool completely until the chocolate hardens. (If I am in a hurry, I put it in the refrigerator. It hardens faster).

Break apart into small pieces.

The matzo will stay fresh in a closed container for 10 days.

Note: I do half the pan with nuts and half without.

/ S'MORE MARSHMALLOW POPS

I found this recipe on the box of Honey Maid Graham Cracker Crumbs. It is so much fun to do with my grandkids...and really a delicious treat!

YIELD: 24   PREHEAT OVEN TO 350 DEGREES

- 24 **Pretzel Sticks (4 inch)**
- 24 **Large Marshmallows**
- 6 **ounces semi-sweet chocolate, melted**
- 2/3 **cup Graham Cracker Crumbs**

Insert one end of each pretzel into a marshmallow bottom Dip Marshmallows in melted chocolate, turning to evenly to coat marshmallows, then dip in graham cracker crumbs.

Place on parchment paper lined pan and refrigerate for 30 minutes

ELEANOR P. BRENNER'S COLD LEMON SOUFFLÉ

Eleanor P. Brenner has become one of the shining stars of 7th avenue and one of our closest friends. Eleanor is known as one of America's leading fashion design-ers. She is also the author of the Gourmet Cooking Without Salt cookbook. This lemon soufflé is one of her favorites and I know it will be one of yours!

- 1¼ cups cold water
- 2 packages unflavored gelatin
- 3⅓ cups heavy cream
- 1 teaspoon vanilla extract (optional)
- 8 large eggs, separated, at room temperature
- 1¾ cups sugar
- ¾ cup lemon juice = juice of 4 large, fresh lemons
- 2 tablespoons lemon rind, finely grated
- ¼ teaspoon cream of tartar

Garnish:
- ⅔ cup heavy cream, whipped with
- 1½ tablespoons confectioners sugar

. . . .

1. Prepare a 2 quart soufflé dish with a 5 inch soufflé collar. Spray the inside with non-stick cooking spray.
2. Place water in the top of a double boiler and sprinkle the gelatin on top of water to soften.
3. Using electric mixer on medium high speed, whip the cream with the vanilla extract until stiff peaks hold their shape. Refrigerate.
4. Fill bottom of double boiler with water to within one inch from top part. Turn flame to medium and bring water to scalding point. Turn the flame low. Place the top part of the double boiler into the bottom and cook for 3 to 4 minutes (water in bottom part should not boil). Turn the flame off.
5. Using an electric mixer on medium speed, beat the egg yolks with the sugar until they are thick, creamy and a pale, yellow color. Slowly add the gelatin mixture, beating all the time, until gelatin is totally absorbed into the egg yolk-sugar-lemon mixture.

ELEANOR P. BRENNER'S
COLD LEMON SOUFFLÉ, cont.

6. In a separate bowl using the electric mixer on high speed, beat the egg whites and cream of tartar until stiff but not dry.
7. Using a rubber spatula, mix ¼ of the egg whites into the egg yolk mixture, then fold in remainder of the egg whites.
8. Fold the whipped cream into the egg mixture.
9. Spoon the mixture into the soufflé dish and refrigerate at least 24 hours.

To serve: Cover the soufflé top with whipped cream, remove collar, serve immediately on a doily covered silver tray.

NIBBLE AND MUNCH

My friend Denise from L.A. gave me this recipe. It's great for a large group of people who like to snack. If you want to make it "sweet", add a cup of M&Ms!

½ cup butter
⅓ cup + ¼ teaspoon Worcestershire sauce
¼ teaspoon garlic powder
¼ teaspoon Mrs. Dash seasoning dash mild chili powder
2 cups of each: Wheat Chex
              Rice Chex
              Cheerios
              thin pretzel sticks
              dry roasted mixed nuts

Melt butter and combine with Worcestershire sauce, garlic powder, Mrs. Dash's seasoning and chili powder.

In a large bowl, combine all the cereals and nuts. Toss with ½ of the seasoning mixture and ½ of cereal. Pour into a 9 x 13 pan. Repeat with other ½ of cereal and seasoning. Toss.

Bake in a 350 degree oven for 45 minutes. Mix while baking.

Cool and store in container. Can also be frozen.

EASY CUCUMBER SAUCE

Cucumber sauce is great on the side of the Salmon Mousse or Salmon Loaf.

2 cups cucumbers, peeled, seeded and chopped
1 cup sour cream
1 tablespoon dill weed (I use fresh)
1 tablespoon chopped chives
½ teaspoon salt

Combine all ingredients and chill.

JAMES GALANOS' FAVORITE RECIPE!

James Galanos is the California Star of American Couture. When my dear friend, Judy Tallarico, asked her good friend Jimmy for his favorite recipe to be included in my cookbook, he replied with a laugh…"I don't cook! I enjoy eating in the newest and most exciting restaurants of the moment." You'll find this recipe easy to follow and a treat to prepare!

CAROLINA HERRERA'S CHOCOLATE MOUSSE

Carolina Herrera has made an outstanding contribution to the field of fashion design. Her creations are chic and elegant. The women who wear her clothes love the way they look and feel. This mousse recipe is delicious! Carolina says "I adore chocolate and enjoy collecting recipes!" Her husband, Reinaldo adds, "My wife is very good at 'giving directions' in the kitchen, but I would not trust her to boil an egg with her own hands."

SERVES 12

- ½ **pound bittersweet chocolate**
- ½ **pound butter**
- 3 **eggs**

Grate chocolate and melt with butter in double boiler. Remove from heat the moment it is melted. Do not allow it to cook. Let cool.

Separate eggs. Beat egg yolks until frothy. Slowly add cooled chocolate and stir well with a wooden spoon.

Beat egg white until firm. Add chocolate mixture, a little at a time, stirring continuously. Pour mixture into 12, 4 ounce pot-de-crèmes. Chill in refrigerator.

This dessert is best prepared the day before serving.

FUN WITH CANDY MELTING CHOCOLATE

Buy any color candy melting chocolate. I buy white chocolate bark that is used for candy making or chocolate discs which I melt in a double boiler or a micro-wave oven. When melted I dip:

Oreo cookies
Pretzels, any kind
Marshmallows, with thin pretzel sticks or sucker sticks as stems
Chocolate wafer cookies

For M&Ms and M&M peanuts, pour candy into chocolate, stir and pour onto wax paper to cool. Then break apart. For an added treat, add crushed Oreo cookies to the mixture.

To display, I take a slab of Styrofoam and take the eraser side of a pencil and stab rows of holes. Then I insert cones so they stand up.

P.S. For a really cute party idea, purchase tiny ice cream cones, with the pointed bottoms, from a candy store. Take a whole marshmallow, cut it in half and place in in opening of cone (like a scoop of ice cream). Dip the cone into melted chocolate so just the marshmallow top is covered. Then sprinkle the wet chocolate with multi-colored non-pareils.

FANCY PLATE DECORATION

Bonnie Rabert, our fabulous food stylist, used this trick to decorate the plate of Caesar Salad Pasta on the cover of the book. She taught me the technique, and I thought I'd pass it on.

Using a plate with at least 1½ inch wide rim, hold a stick of butter like a felt-tip pen and use it to coat rim. Use about ½ teaspoon of butter. Place a piece of wax paper under plate. Sprinkle rim with 1½ tablespoons of appropriate garnish. Turn plate while sprinkling to get even coverage.

Clean exterior edge of plate with paper towel to give a finished, even look

Garnish options:
- parsley
- Parmesan cheese
- breadcrumbs
- paprika
- cocoa

/ PASTA "CRUST"

½   cup freshly grated Parmesan-Reggiano cheese
1   cup Panko bread crumbs
2½   tablespoons olive oil
    salt and pepper, to taste

Toss the bread crumbs with cheese, oil, salt and pepper.

Sprinkle this on top of any pasta dish that is cooked. Broil the dish till the top is browned.

ELLIE'S PARTY PITA BREAD

These little "pick-ups" are great as appetizers or served with a main course.

- 1 package Pita bread
- ¼ pound butter, softened
  Parmesan cheese
  grated garlic powder
  oregano
  sesame seeds

Cut pita bread into two round pieces. Cut each half into quarters. Lightly spread soft side of bread with butter. Sprinkle with Parmesan cheese and garlic powder. If desired, sprinkle with oregano and/or sesame seeds.

Place under broiler, until just brown and bubbly. Watch carefully to prevent burning. Serve warm. These toasts can be kept for 3 days if put into an air-tight container.

HERB PULL APART BREAD

No one will believe you made this bread. It is an added accessory to any dinner.

PREHEAT OVEN TO 325 DEGREES

- 2 Pillsbury cans of rolls
- 2 packets of dry good seasonings or Italian seasoning
- ⅓ cup chopped basil
- ⅓ cup chopped parsley
- 1 cup butter, melted

Spray a bundt pan with non-stick cooking spray.

Cut rolls into quarters and roll in seasonings (dry and fresh). Drop them into the prepared pan. Drizzle melted butter over the seasoned rolls. Bake for 30 minutes in a preheated 325 degree oven.

Invert onto a plate. This is best served right out of the oven.

/ELEGANT FRUIT AND CHAMPAGNE SOUP

This is a very special, delicious way to start any dinner party. My guests love it!

- 1 cup sparking wine or champagne (I love to use pink)
- 2 cups cantaloupe, chopped
- 2 cups honey dew, chopped
- 2 cups watermelon, seeded and cut into pieces
- ½ cup orange juice
- ½ cup lime juice
- ½ cup apricot nectar
- ½ cup lemon yogurt

Blend all ingredients together. Chill for at least 4 hours. Serve with small pieces of melon or berries to garnish.

MARK HEISTER'S COLD CUCUMBER SOUP

Chicago's own dapper designer Mark Heister not only creates timeless ensembles, but leads his day to day life as a Renaissance man. He's made his mark in the fashion world not only as a Gold Coast Fashion awardee but was also honored by the Chicago Historical Society in a one man retrospective of his fashions.

SERVES 4

- 2 tablespoons butter
- ¼ cup onion, chopped
- OR
- 1 leek, unpeeled and diced
- 1 cup watercress leaves, chopped
- ½ cup potato, finely diced
- 2 cups chicken broth
- 2 sprigs parsley
- ¼ teaspoon salt
- ¼ teaspoon ground pepper
- ¼ teaspoon dry mustard
- 1 cup heavy cream

Garnish: chives, chopped
cucumbers, chopped
radishes, chopped

In sauce pan melt butter. Add onion and cook until transparent. Add all remaining ingredients except cream and garnish vegetables and bring to boil. Simmer fifteen minutes or until potatoes are tender.

Puree in electric blender or put mixture through food mill and, if desired, through sieve or cheesecloth. Add more seasonings to taste. Chill in refrigerator.

Before serving, stir in cream. Garnish with chives, cucumber and radishes. Soup will be thick. It is suggested that it be served in parfait glasses with radish roses and garnishes.

/DIET CHINESE VEGGIE SOUP

When I became a widow, I needed something to eat that was warm, welcoming and filling - but not fattening. I could make a large pot of this soup and have it for many meals. It became my "go-to" choice! I still love it!

1	32 ounce container of low fat, low sodium chicken broth
1	8 ounce can water chestnuts, drained and sliced
20	pea pods, cut in half
20	mushrooms, sliced
6	small to medium shrimp, cut in bite size pieces
1	raw chicken breast
½	cup celery, roughly chopped
	salt and pepper, optional

Heat all ingredients in a large pot. Simmer for 20-30 minutes, or until all meats are cooked through and the vegetables are tender. Shred the chicken meat and serve.

P.S. if you are short on time, you can add cooked chicken instead of raw.

/ HEARTY TURKEY CHILI

1 pound ground turkey
1 onion, chopped
1 15 ounce can white navy beans, drained
1 15 ounce can red kidney beans, drained
1 15 ounce can garbanzo beans, drained
1 package chili seasoning (Lawry's or McCormick's)
2 8 ounce cans petite diced tomatoes
Garnish: cheddar cheese, shredded (optional)
      sour cream (optional)
      chopped onions (optional)

In a large pot, brown the turkey with the chopped onion. Drain the pan of the excess liquids. Add all the remaining ingredients and cook for 20 minutes.

I love to serve this chili in taco bowls. Chili seasoning comes in mild, medium and spicy. This chili is delicious at any spice level!

ELLEN'S "STAFF OF LIFE"

Here's a recipe that's quick, cheap, delicious, healthy and portable. Ellen says, "You can eat as much as you like and still fit into your Scaasi's, Mackie's, Galanos' – or favorite pair of blue jeans!"

    1   cup popcorn, preferably blue corn or "Black Diamond"
    3   tablespoons vegetable oil
        popcorn salt

....

In a 3 quart saucepan, heat oil to 400 degrees. Add popcorn, cover and shake vigorously for 3 minutes, or until popping ceases. Immediately remove from heat and pour into large bowl. Cool, then sprinkle with popcorn salt.

DON'T EVEN THINK ABOUT BUTTERING IT.

Serve with a Diet Coke.

VANILLA SAUCE

This recipe is a delicious topping for fancy soufflés and simple brownies.

YIELD ½ CUPS

- ½ cup butter
- 1 cup sugar
- ½ cup light cream
- 1 teaspoon vanilla extract

Melt butter in medium saucepan. Remove from heat. Add sugar, cream and vanilla. Mix well. Simmer over low heat for 5 minutes. Keep stirring until sugar is dissolved and sauce is heated through. Serve immediately.

CHOCOLATE SOUFFLÉ

When we were first married, Barry used to make this dessert whenever we entertained.

SERVES 6-8 PREHEAT OVEN TO 425 DEGREES

- 4 tablespoons butter
- ¼ cup sugar, for coating casserole
- 1 cup milk
- 2 1 ounce squares unsweetened chocolate
- ⅓ cup flour
- ¼ teaspoon salt
- 4 eggs, separated
- ⅓ cup sugar
- 1 teaspoon vanilla extract
- ¼ teaspoon almond extract
- whipped cream, for garnish
- Vanilla Sauce, for garnish (see recipe)

....

Liberally grease 1½ quart casserole with butter. Sprinkle bottom and sides with sugar until just coated.

In double boiler, heat ½ cup milk with chocolate. Stir until melted. Beat until smooth with egg beater. In a separate bowl, mix flour, salt and remainder of milk.

Stir into chocolate. Continue stirring and cook over medium heat until mixture is very thick. Remove from heat and beat until smooth.

Add egg yolks, one at a time, beating after each addition. Cover and set aside. With electric mixer, beat egg whites until small peaks form. Slowly add ⅓ cup sugar and continue to beat until stiff. Fold in chocolate mixture and extracts. Pour into prepared casserole.

Bake in a preheated 425 degree oven for 20-30 minutes. To test for doneness, poke a knife ½ way down in center of soufflé. Knife should come out dry.

Serve immediately with whipped cream or Vanilla Sauce on the side.

COLD STRAWBERRY SOUP

SERVES 4

  3 cups strawberries, washed – cut off stems
1½ cups water
1½ cups white wine
 ½ cup sugar
  2 tablespoons fresh lemon juice
1½ teaspoons corn starch
1½ tablespoons cold water
  3 teaspoons lemon rind, grated
 ½ cup sour cream
     fresh strawberries, for garnish

Thinly slice strawberries. Place in 3 quart saucepan. Combine with water and wine. Cover and simmer for 10 minutes. Add sugar and lemon juice. Stir to blend. Combine corn starch with cold water. Pour into mixture and blend well. Over medium heat, bring to a boil. Stir just until thickened.

Pour into blender. Add lemon rind and sour cream. Whip until light pink in color. Cool completely. Add additional sugar to taste. Chill in refrigerator four hours or overnight. Stir to blend before serving. Pour into individual bowls and top with fresh sliced strawberries. A delicious summer treat!

MARLEY'S SWEET BAR-B-QUE SAUCE

This delicious sauce was given to me by one of my testers, Marley Stein. It's an old family recipe that was handed down to her. She was so "sweet" to share it with me! This recipe can easily be doubled or tripled. It keeps in the refrigerator up to one month.

  1   12 ounce bottle chili sauce
  ½   bottle water
  ½   cup brown sugar
  1   medium onion, diced
  ⅛   cup vinegar
  ⅛   cup Worcestershire sauce
      salt to taste
      pepper to taste
      garlic powder to taste
      paprika to taste

Pour chili sauce in a medium saucepan. Using emptied bottle, fill half full with water. Shake to pick up leftover sauce and pour into saucepan. Add brown sugar, onion, vinegar, and Worcestershire sauce. Sprinkle salt, pepper, garlic powder and paprika to taste. Mix well, and simmer 30–40 minutes. Stir occasionally.

Cool and store in refrigerator. Great on chicken and ribs! Be sure to brush on sauce at end of grilling time. Watch closely to prevent burning.

HERBED FRESH TOMATO SOUP

This soup makes a beautiful presentation at an elegant dinner party, It's also a favorite when served plain at a family dinner.

SERVES 8

- 2 tablespoons butter
- 2 tablespoons olive oil
- 2 medium onions, thinly sliced
- 1 6 ounce can tomato paste
- 2 tablespoons fresh basil, chopped
- 4 tablespoons fresh thyme, chopped
- 2 pounds fresh tomatoes, peeled, seeded, quartered (approximately 5 cups)
- 3 cups chicken broth
- 1 teaspoon salt
- ⅛ teaspoon pepper
- 2 packets artificial sweetener
  whipped cream
  fresh thyme or basil, chopped

In large saucepan, combine butter and olive oil. Over medium heat, cook until butter melts. Add onions and cook until tender, but not brown. Stir in tomato paste, basil and thyme. Mash fresh tomatoes and add to mixture. Pour in chicken broth. Mix well.

Bring to a boil. Reduce heat and cover. Simmer for 40 minutes. Press through food mill, sieve or puree in blender.

Return soup to saucepan. Stir in salt, pepper and sweetener. Heat to serve. Pour into individual bowls and garnish with dollop of whipped cream. Sprinkle with pinch of chopped herbs.

This makes a delicious light meal when accompanied by a tossed salad and garlic bread.

MAUREEN'S SPAGHETTI SAUCE

This delicious, full-bodied sauce is a family recipe passed down to my friend Maureen Kotler. It's terrific on pasta, grilled veal chops or baked eggplant!

3	pounds ground meat
2	tablespoons garlic, minced
1	pound medium onions
3-4	green peppers, chopped
1	pound fresh mushrooms, sliced
2	8 ounce cans whole tomatoes
2	8 ounce cans tomato sauce
2	8 ounce cans stewed tomatoes
3	packages dry spaghetti sauce mix
½	cup sugar
⅓	cup parsley, chopped
1½	teaspoons Accent
1½	teaspoons salt
1½	teaspoons Italian seasoning
1	teaspoon garlic powder
1	teaspoon allspice
1	teaspoon nutmeg
1	teaspoon pepper
1	small can tomato paste for thickening

In a large frying pan, brown meat with garlic, onions, green peppers and mushrooms. Drain all fat. Add canned tomatoes, tomato sauce, stewed tomatoes and dry spaghetti sauce mix. Stir to blend well. Add rest of ingredients. Simmer for 90 minutes, uncovered, stirring occasionally. Add tomato paste to thicken.

This sauce freezes well.

JANET'S FROTHY FINALE

Janet Newman has been my good friend for a very long time. She is famous for wearing fresh flowers in her hair. She should also be famous for this delicious recipe.

SERVES 4-6

- 1 pint lemon sherbet, softened
- 1 pint pineapple sherbet, softened
- 1 pint French vanilla ice cream, softened
- DO NOT SUBSTITUTE ice milk or frozen yogurt
- 1½ tablespoons grated lemon zest (2 lemons)
- 1 tablespoon Cointreau
- 1 tablespoon Grand Marnier
- 2 1 ounce squares semi-sweet chocolate, finely grated
- 2 1 ounce squares milk chocolate, finely grated
- small fresh flowers, for garnish (optional)
- mint leaves, for garnish (optional)

. . . .

Blend sherbets and ice cream until creamy. Add grated lemon zest and blend well. Add Cointreau and Grand Marnier, adding more to taste. Stir until well blended. Pour into small mixing bowl and cover. Put in freezer for several hours or overnight.

Remove from freezer 30 minutes before serving. Beat into frothy texture. Spoon into individual champagne flutes or parfait glasses. Form top into peak and top with a sprinkling of both chocolates. Garnish with a fresh flower and a mint leaf.

ILENE AND STEVE'S HOT FUDGE

SERVES 4 - 6

- ½   cup granulated sugar
- 2   1-ounce squares semi-sweet chocolate
- 4   tablespoons milk
- 2   tablespoons dark corn syrup
- ¼   teaspoon vanilla extract
- 2   tablespoons butter

Place all ingredients in small saucepan and cook on low-medium heat. Slowly stir with rubber or wooden spoon and continue to cook until all chocolate has been melted. Bring to a slow boil and continue to cook and stir until desired thickness (the longer it cooks the thicker it becomes). Serve over your favorite ice cream.

BOB MACKIE'S LATE NIGHT PIG OUT!

Bob Mackie is known as the "King of Glitter!" His gorgeous gowns are sought after by the biggest names in Hollywood. In fact, there isn't a woman who doesn't feel glamorous in one of his fabulous creations! Bob says, "this is the recipe that made me what I am today."

1. Take one half pint of Haagen Daaz "Vanilla Swiss Almond" ice cream.
2. Sit down in front of TV.
3. Open carton and eat with large spoon
4. Finish the entire contents.

LIST OF RECIPES

INDEX

APPETIZERS

BARS

BREADS

BROWNIES

CAKES

CANDY

CHOCOLATE

COFFEE

COOKIES

DECORATIONS

Chocolate Filigree Garnish

Fancy Plate Decoration..........263

DESIGNERS

MEATS

PIES

POPCORN

POULTRY

QUICHE

SALADS

SAUCES

SEAFOOD

SOUFFLÉS

SOUPS

VEGETABLES

Made in the USA
Middletown, DE
12 May 2015